GEORGE WASHINGTON

An American Life

Laurie Calkoven

Sterling Publishing Co., Inc.
New York

For my grandparents, who became Americans,
and my parents, who taught me how important that was.

Library of Congress Cataloging-in-Publication Data

Calkhoven, Laurie.
George Washington : an American life / Laurie Calkhoven.
p. cm. -- (Sterling biographies)
Includes bibliographical references and index.
ISBN-13: 978-1-4027-3546-2
ISBN-10: 1-4027-3546-4
1. Washington, George, 1732-1799--Juvenile literature. 2. Presidents--United States--Biography--Juvenile literature. I. Title.

E312.66.C28 2007
973.4'1092--dc22
[B]

2006027362

10 9 8 7 6 5 4 3 2 1

Published by Sterling Publishing Co., Inc.
387 Park Avenue South, New York, NY 10016

Distributed in Canada by Sterling Publishing
c/o Canadian Manda Group, 165 Dufferin Street
Toronto, Ontario, Canada M6K 3H6
Distributed in the United Kingdom by GMC Distribution Services
Castle Place, 166 High Street, Lewes, East Sussex, England BN7 1XU
Distributed in Australia by Capricorn Link (Australia) Pty. Ltd.
P.O. Box 704, Windsor, NSW 2756, Australia

Printed in China

Sterling ISBN-13: 978-1-4027-3546-2 (paperback)
ISBN-10: 1-4027-3546-4

Sterling ISBN-13: 978-1-4027-4748-9 (hardcover)
ISBN-10: 1-4027-4748-9

Designed by Joe Borzetta
Image research by Susan Schader

For information about custom editions, special sales, premium and corporate purchases, please contact Sterling Special Sales Department at 800-805-5489 or specialsales@sterlingpub.com.

Contents

Events in the Life of George Washington

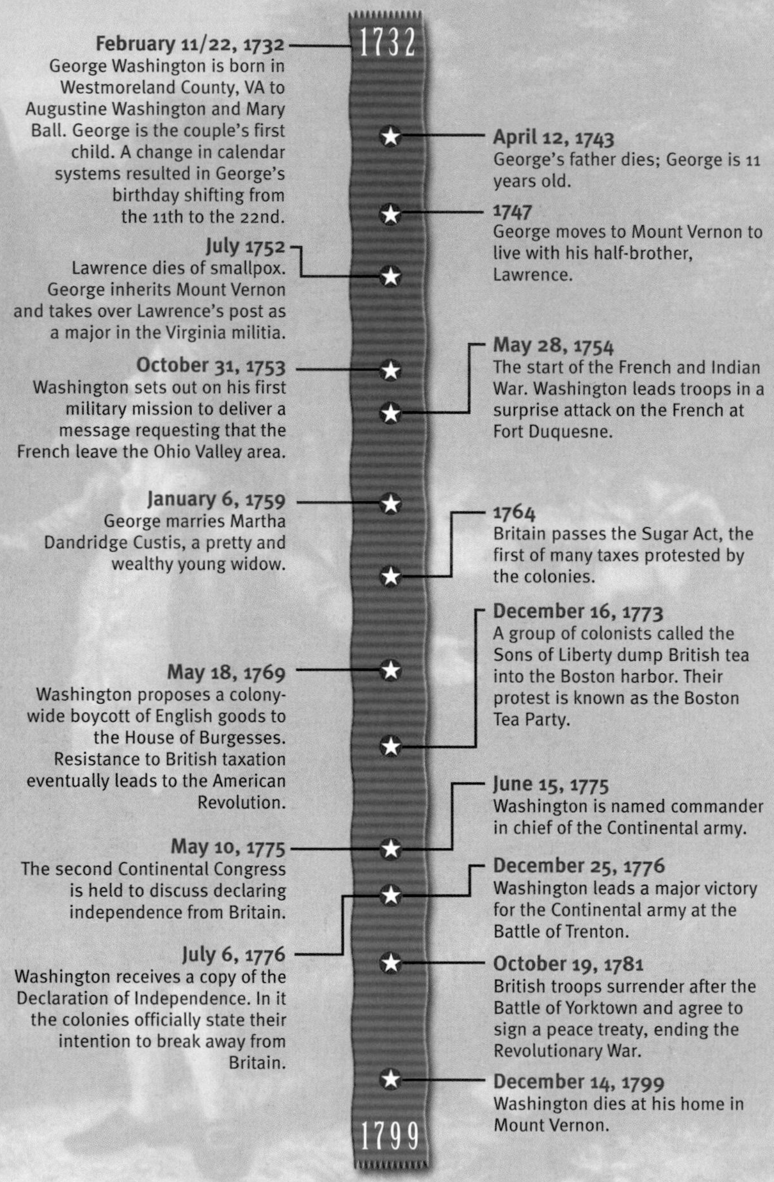

February 11/22, 1732
George Washington is born in Westmoreland County, VA to Augustine Washington and Mary Ball. George is the couple's first child. A change in calendar systems resulted in George's birthday shifting from the 11th to the 22nd.

April 12, 1743
George's father dies; George is 11 years old.

1747
George moves to Mount Vernon to live with his half-brother, Lawrence.

July 1752
Lawrence dies of smallpox. George inherits Mount Vernon and takes over Lawrence's post as a major in the Virginia militia.

October 31, 1753
Washington sets out on his first military mission to deliver a message requesting that the French leave the Ohio Valley area.

May 28, 1754
The start of the French and Indian War. Washington leads troops in a surprise attack on the French at Fort Duquesne.

January 6, 1759
George marries Martha Dandridge Custis, a pretty and wealthy young widow.

1764
Britain passes the Sugar Act, the first of many taxes protested by the colonies.

May 18, 1769
Washington proposes a colony-wide boycott of English goods to the House of Burgesses. Resistance to British taxation eventually leads to the American Revolution.

December 16, 1773
A group of colonists called the Sons of Liberty dump British tea into the Boston harbor. Their protest is known as the Boston Tea Party.

May 10, 1775
The second Continental Congress is held to discuss declaring independence from Britain.

June 15, 1775
Washington is named commander in chief of the Continental army.

July 6, 1776
Washington receives a copy of the Declaration of Independence. In it the colonies officially state their intention to break away from Britain.

December 25, 1776
Washington leads a major victory for the Continental army at the Battle of Trenton.

October 19, 1781
British troops surrender after the Battle of Yorktown and agree to sign a peace treaty, ending the Revolutionary War.

December 14, 1799
Washington dies at his home in Mount Vernon.

An American Life

First in war, first in peace, and first in the hearts of his countrymen.

—Henry "Light-Horse Harry" Lee

When you think about George Washington, you probably think of the stern-looking face of the old man on the dollar bill. And, of course, you know that George Washington was the first president of the United States.

But did you know that at the age of fourteen, Washington tried to join the British navy? Americans might have lost the Revolutionary War if George Washington had gone away to sea. Luckily for us, his mother didn't let him.

Instead of going abroad, George Washington went into the American wilderness. He became a **surveyor**, helping map out the frontiers of Virginia. Later, he joined the Virginia **militia** and fought with the British in the French and Indian War.

Washington's early experiences in the wilderness and in the war were two important reasons why he was the man who could lead the ragtag **Continental army** against the British in the American Revolution. He had the wisdom, the courage, and the following among the American people to lead thirteen different states into nationhood and help form the United States of America.

CHAPTER 1

A Virginia Childhood

I can read three or four pages sometimes without missing a word. Ma says I may go to see you, and stay all day with you next week if it be not rainy.

At a time when many of the people living in the colonies were either new immigrants or the first people in their families to be born in America, George Washington was a fourth-generation Virginian. His great-grandfather, John Washington, was an English adventurer who crossed the Atlantic Ocean as a shipmate.

John landed in Virginia in 1657 and married the daughter of a wealthy tobacco farmer. He had a passion for land—lots of land. His bride's father gave the couple seven hundred acres as a wedding gift, and soon after they married, John obtained even more. Some he bought, some he simply claimed. The Seneca Indians named him *Conotocarius*, which meant "town taker," or "devourer of villages," not because he was a great warrior, but because he used the law to swindle them out of their land. In Virginia society, John and his family had a different reputation. Even though they were never among the richest plantation owners in the colony, they became respected members.

Born on February 11?

When George Washington was born, England and its colonies were using the Julian calendar. The Julian calendar gained one day about every 134 years, so it was replaced with the Gregorian calendar by the sixteenth century. But England refused to accept the Gregorian calendar until 1752, almost two hundred years after other parts of the world. By that time, the two calendars had a difference of eleven days. Washington's birthday moved from February 11 to February 22.

Did Washington give up his original birthday? Maybe not. On February 11, 1799, shortly before he died, Washington wrote in his journal, "went up to Alexandria to the celebration of my birthday." So, evidence suggests that Washington continued to celebrate his birthday on February 11, not February 22.

George Washington's grandfather and his father, both tobacco farmers, added to the family's land. Washington's father, Augustine Washington, bought the land along the Potomac River that would one day be called Mount Vernon. Like his own father and grandfather, Augustine became a justice of the county court.

Augustine Washington married twice. His first wife died in 1729 and left him with three children—George's half brothers Lawrence and

Much of the Washington family money came from growing tobacco. The leaves of the tobacco plant, like the one shown here, are cured for smoking, chewing, and sniffing.

Augustine, Jr., and his half sister, Jane. Two years later, Augustine married Mary Ball and they had six children—George was the oldest. He was born on his father's plantation on February 11, 1732, in Westmoreland County, Virginia. Very little is known about George Washington's childhood, but there were tragedies early on in his life, and he must have known sadness at a young age. When he was a toddler, Jane, his half sister, died. Another sister, Mildred, died when she was just one year old.

In 1735, Augustine Washington moved his family to a house on a bluff at Little Hunting Creek Plantation on the Potomac. In 1738, when George was six, the family moved again. Their new home, Ferry Farm, was on the banks of the Rappahannock River, across from Fredericksburg.

Fredericksburg was a busy town, and Ferry Farm must have been a lively place. Ships came across the ocean and sailed up the Rappahannock to Fredericksburg, right past George's windows. A ferryboat brought people from the Washington property to the town. There was a steady stream of visitors to the Washington home.

Although there aren't many written records of George's life on Ferry Farm, we know that he sometimes exchanged letters and books with a friend named Richard Henry Lee who lived nearby. In a letter George

George Washington spent some of his earliest years in this house called Ferry Farm.

wrote to Richard when he was nine, he promised a visit "if it be not rainy." George probably trotted along on his father's daily rounds of the plantation on horseback, and he must have explored the forest surrounding the farm. George became an expert horseman and developed a love of the wilderness.

A Colonial Education

Boys in the Virginia colony usually began their education around the age of seven. Lessons in reading, writing, and arithmetic came first. Later on, they were often taught Latin and Greek, along with practical subjects like geometry and

bookkeeping. George may have gone to school in nearby Fredericksburg, or studied with a private tutor. Math was his favorite subject.

Virginia planters, like George's father, often sent their sons to England for school when they were old enough. George's half brothers, Lawrence and Augustine, Jr., had studied in England, and that was Augustine's plan for George. But that arrangement changed drastically when George was eleven years old and tragedy struck the family again. George's father died, and there wasn't enough money to send George to an English boarding school.

Augustine Washington left most of his estate to George's half brothers. George's part of the inheritance was Ferry Farm, along with ten of Augustine's twenty slaves. His mother, Mary Ball, was supposed to have control of the farm until George turned twenty-one, but she never gave up George's inheritance and lived on Ferry Farm until near the end of her life.

George's mother put him in charge of his younger brothers and sisters. She was very strict, and she scolded George and his siblings often, making it difficult for them to live with her. Even after George led the Continental army to victory and became president of the United States, Mary Ball criticized him for not visiting her enough. She once wrote to him on the eve of an important battle during the French and Indian War to tell him that she needed butter!

Mary Bell Washington was hard on her son, George. His friends were afraid of her.

Slavery

How could a man like George Washington, who fought for liberty, also own slaves? This is hard for us to understand today.

Washington was born at a time when slavery was accepted, and he did not question it. In order to be profitable, tobacco plantations in Virginia, and all other plantations in the South, relied on slaves for cheap labor. As Washington traveled around the country and fought for liberty in the Revolution, his views about slavery began to change. By the time he became president, he held the belief that slavery was wrong, and when he died, he included in his will that all his slaves were to be freed (see chapter 14).

When George was fifteen he moved to the farm that his brother Lawrence had renamed Mount Vernon, where he continued his education by reading. At one point he copied instructions from the book *Rules of Civility and Decent Behaviour in Company and Conversation* into his diary. Although he may have just been practicing his penmanship, the first rule, which states, "Every action done in company ought to be done with some sign of respect to those that are present," seems to have stayed with him forever. George also continued to teach himself math and science. He educated himself throughout his life, but he always regretted not going to college.

Chapter 2

Early Adventures

Went into the bed, as they called it, when to my surprise, I found it to be nothing but a little straw matted together without sheet or anything else, but only one threadbare blanket with double its weight of vermin, such as lice, fleas, etc., and I was glad to get up.

After his father died, George found a substitute father in his half brother Lawrence, who was fourteen years older than George. George looked up to his big brother and Lawrence offered George affection and guidance.

Lawrence was an officer in an American regiment that fought with the British against the Spanish. He inspired his younger brother with a passion for military life, and George started to dream of having a career in the British military.

Even more important in shaping George's newfound love of the army was his introduction, through Lawrence, to the powerful

Lawrence Washington named Mount Vernon after British Admiral Edward Vernon, whom Lawrence served with and admired.

Fairfax family. Lord Thomas Fairfax lived in England, but owned a huge portion of the Virginia colony—land granted to him by the British king. Lord Fairfax's agent in America, William Fairfax (who was also his cousin), took a liking to George and introduced him to life as a member of the British aristocracy.

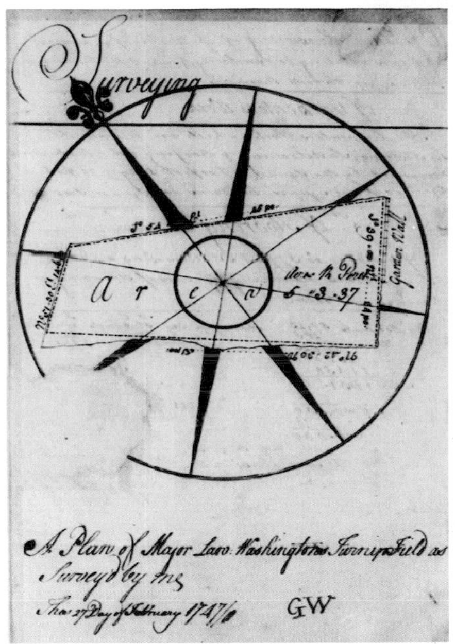

George took to surveying at an early age. He drew this surveying diagram for his brother when he was only ten years old.

George loved the elegance of Belvoir, the Fairfax home that bordered Mount Vernon, and he especially loved foxhunting. George was an expert horseman, and he drew the attention of Lord Fairfax when he visited from England.

Lord Fairfax used his power to win George a spot as a midshipman in the British navy. George's bags were packed and he was ready to go, but at the last minute, his mother said no. Either because she didn't want George to leave her, or because she had learned that Americans were badly treated by English officers, George had to unpack his bags and stay in Virginia.

Still, he longed for adventure. In 1748, William Fairfax gave sixteen-year-old George his first job. George went with William's son, George William Fairfax, on a surveying trip of the Fairfaxes' property in the wilderness of the Shenandoah Valley. They had to

As a boy, George Washington loved to visit his half brother Lawrence at Mount Vernon and later lived with him there.

map and measure the land and set boundaries. To get there, they had to cross the Blue Ridge Mountains.

Along the way, George was surprised by the conditions in some of the inns. He wrote in his journal about the "vermin, such as lice and fleas" that he found in the blankets. He was much happier sleeping outside under the stars. The settlers he met on the frontier seemed strange and tough in their tattered clothes. Most of them spoke German instead of English.

The trip took thirty-one days, and it was a thrilling experience. George learned surveying, swam horses across rivers swollen with melted snow, got lost in the mountains, and stumbled across a rattlesnake. He also met a party of Indians carrying a scalp, and George even witnessed the Indians performing a war dance.

Mapping the Virginia Wilderness

George loved the adventure, and he needed a job. He certainly never went hungry, but he was ashamed to entertain his new friends at the run-down Ferry Farm. So, at the age of seventeen, with the help of the Fairfax family, George was named surveyor of Culpeper County. It was his first public office.

George became an expert surveyor over the next three years by doing more than 190 surveys on Virginia's frontiers. He mostly camped under the stars and was toughened up by the wilderness. He worked hard and saved his money.

Like his great-grandfather John Washington, and his father and grandfather, George had a passion for land. By the time he was eighteen, George had earned enough money to buy his first plot—almost fifteen hundred acres on Bullskin Creek, a tributary of the Shenandoah River.

Surveying

It's hard to believe now, but in George Washington's time there were just a few cities, no roads, and almost no maps. Dirt paths connected the colonies. Surveyors relied on old Indian trails to make their way into the wilderness, and often had to carve their own paths. Using a chain measure made up of one hundred flexible links and a compass, surveyors measured land, marked property boundaries, and drew maps. It was the perfect job for someone like George Washington, who loved math, horses, and the outdoors.

A brass surveyor's compass

Sally Cary Fairfax

George Washington fell in love with Sally Cary Fairfax when he was sixteen and she was the eighteen-year-old bride of his good friend and fellow adventurer George William Fairfax.

When he fell for Sally, George fell hard. She considered George to be a great friend, but because she was already married, she did not return his love. Eventually, Sally and her husband became good friends with George and, later, with his wife, Martha. The Fairfaxes were the closest neighbors to Mount Vernon, and they visited regularly. Still, near the end of his life, George wrote to Sally about their moments together so many years before—before the long French and Indian War and the even longer American Revolution. He called those moments spent with Sally "the happiest in my life."

George kept a diary of his adventures. He kept a diary for most of his life, recording things such as whether or not it rained and how far he rode on his horse. Later on, his diary would be about what kinds of crops he planted or how many soldiers he commanded. As a young man, George also wrote some very bad love poems.

Although he was an excellent dancer and horseman, George was unlucky with girls. He was shy and quiet, and they might have been a little afraid of him. At a time when most men were shorter than five feet five inches, George stood at least six feet two inches tall. His reddish brown hair (worn in a ponytail) and gray-blue eyes would have towered over anyone who came near. He also had huge hands and feet.

George forgot all about love poetry when tragedy struck again. His beloved brother Lawrence caught tuberculosis, a lung disease, and he was dying. Together, the brothers sailed for the island of Barbados in search of a cure. George was finally able to go to sea. It was his one and only trip outside of America, but it was a sad one because Lawrence did not get better.

While in Barbados, George spent time with British officers and toured some of the biggest fortifications in the British colonies. George himself became sick with smallpox, a very contagious disease. He recovered, although the virus left a few scars on his nose. But from then on, due to his infection and recovery, George was immune to the most deadly disease of the times and the greatest killer during the American Revolution.

Although he was an excellent dancer and horseman, George was unlucky with girls. He was shy and quiet, and they might have been a little afraid of him.

Lawrence returned to home to die. Shortly after his death in 1752, George inherited Mount Vernon. William Fairfax used his power with the governor to make sure that George took over Lawrence's post as a major in the Virginia militia, which was to be George's first step in a long military career. Although George had no military experience and no qualifications for the job, he was an impressive young man and a natural leader.

Chapter 3

Washington the Soldier

I heard the bullets whistle, and, believe me, there is something charming in the sound.

There were settlers from many European nations in North America during George Washington's time. Most of them came from France and England. The English settlers—more than a million of them—were mostly farmers. Almost all of them lived in the thirteen colonies. The French—less than one hundred thousand—were mostly traders with settlements in Quebec.

The English claimed all the land along the Atlantic seaboard. The French claimed the Great Lakes area, the Mississippi Valley, and all the land west of the Appalachian Mountains. Both England and France believed that the land in the Ohio Valley belonged to them.

In 1753, the lieutenant governor of Virginia, Robert Dinwiddie, learned that French troops had moved south from Canada and were building forts in the Ohio Valley. When Dinwiddie reported this news to King George II in England, the king ordered Dinwiddie to build a fort to protect English land. He also wanted a messenger to go and warn the French that they had to move out of the Ohio Valley.

The governor needed a Virginian who

Robert Dinwiddie was the highest ranking English official in Virginia.

knew how to navigate through the wilderness and could travel to the French positions and back before the worst of the winter weather set in. He also needed a leader who could act on behalf of the king. There was just one man who fit the bill: twenty-one-year-old George Washington.

A Dangerous Mission

Washington set out in October, 1753, with two interpreters and four backwoodsmen. It was a dangerous five-hundred-mile mission through snow-covered mountains and Indian-filled forests. When the group arrived at the Ohio Valley, Washington dashed ahead. For two days he explored the area alone, searching for the best place to build a fort. He settled on the fork of the Ohio River. Washington had no real military experience, but he chose wisely. The fort would have command of the two rivers that came together—the Allegheny and the Monongahela—and would be easy to protect. Both the French and the British would later built forts on that very spot. Today, it is the city of Pittsburgh, Pennsylvania.

Washington then met an Iroquois chief called the Half King, who gave Washington the name *Conotocarius*, or "town taker," after his great grandfather John. The Half-King, a friend of the British, joined Washington on his mission.

Two months after he began his journey, Washington and his party finally reached the French at Fort Le Boeuf on French Creek. The fort was surrounded by water and cannons. Washington delivered his message on behalf of King George II, warning the French that they had to leave English land. The French commander replied: "As to the summons you send me to retire, I do not think myself obliged to obey it," and believing the

French were entitled to claim the land as theirs, the commander did not try to hide the more than two hundred canoes that were ready to take his troops down to the Forks of the Ohio in the spring.

Washington had his answer, but his mission was only half over. It had taken him longer than he expected to reach the French. It was already mid-December, and he still had to make it back to Virginia. His return home was an even wilder adventure than his journey to meet the French.

A deep freeze had set in. Icy water turned so cold that it burned the men's mouths when they tried to drink it. Rivers and creeks were full of chunks of ice, making it impossible to cross them. The trails were almost as bad. The horses' legs sank into snowdrifts and were cut by crusts of ice. The group moved slower and slower.

Both men were cold and hungry, and the river seemed impossible to cross.

In a hurry to warn the lieutenant governor of a possible French attack, Washington and his Indian translator, Christopher Gist, pushed ahead on foot. An Indian guide promised to lead them on a shortcut where there was no path. The three men trudged through dark, ice-covered forest. When they came to a clearing, the Indian ran ahead, turned, and shot at Washington and Gist. Maybe the guide was on the side of the French, or maybe he simply didn't like the British. We'll never know, but it was the first time a bullet was aimed directly at Washington, and it missed. It wouldn't be the last.

Washington stopped the Indian before he could reload. Gist wanted to execute him, but Washington didn't want to see a man

Christopher Gist and George Washington crossing the Allegheny River

killed. The Indian was sent in one direction, while Washington and Gist ran in another. Afraid that the Indian would come back with a war party, they walked through the icy wilderness for two days without stopping to light a campfire.

Finally they came to the Monongahela River. It wasn't frozen over as they hoped it would be. Huge chunks of ice rushed by in the current. Washington and Gist managed to build a flimsy raft, but the ice threatened to smash it into pieces. Washington was thrown into the river. He managed to climb back on board, but his wet clothes froze solid. Eventually, the two men struggled onto a small island in the middle of the river.

Their situation seemed hopeless, as Washington fell into a restless sleep. Both men were cold and hungry, and the river seemed impossible to cross. But Washington woke at dawn to a wonderful sight. Overnight, the river had frozen solid into a sheet of glass. The two men were able to cross the frozen river and head back to civilization.

The governor was grateful for and impressed with Washington's adventure. He urged Washington to write a record of the expedition. *The Journal of Major George Washington* was published and appeared in colonial newspapers and in magazines in England and Scotland. The young soldier was suddenly famous.

THE
JOURNAL
OF
Major *George Washington*,
SENT BY THE
Hon. *ROBERT DINWIDDIE*, Esq;
His Majesty's Lieutenant-Governor, and
Commander in Chief of *VIRGINIA*,
TO THE
COMMANDANT
OF THE
FRENCH FORCES
ON
OHIO.
TO WHICH ARE ADDED, THE
GOVERNOR's LETTER;
AND A TRANSLATION OF THE
FRENCH OFFICER's ANSWER.
WILLIAMSBURG:
Printed by WILLIAM HUNTER. 1754.

The Journal of Major George Washington

Opening Shots

A few months later, the governor convinced the Virginia legislature to build an army of three hundred men to tell the French again that they had to leave the Ohio Valley. Washington was mentioned as a possible commander. He had never led men in battle, and the French were strong opponents. Washington knew he wasn't ready, so he asked to be named second in command.

An advance team discovered that the French had already reached the Forks of the Ohio. Rumors of a French invasion reached the governor, and he ordered Washington to go over the mountains. In April 1754, Washington headed west with the 159 soldiers that had been enlisted so far. Washington's commander never caught up, and the twenty-two-year-old found himself leading a very small army.

Washington continued his advance, even though news had reached him that his troops were greatly outnumbered by the French and their Indian allies. There were also Indians who supported the British, like the Half-King, and Washington did not want to let them, or the British, down.

The Half-King reported that a party of French soldiers was in the woods nearby. England and France were not yet at war. Even though the French had not attacked, and Washington had been ordered to warn them away before fighting, he led a surprise raid against them.

Washington crept through a dark, rainy night with forty soldiers and a group of Indians. They surrounded the campsite of thirty-two French soldiers. At dawn, Washington led the surprise attack. He did not know it at the time, but these were the first shots in a war that would last seven years.

At dawn, Washington led the surprise attack. He did not know it at the time, but these were the first shots in a war that would last seven years.

Victory was quick. It was Washington's first taste of battle and he was fearless. "I heard the bullets whistle," he wrote to his brother, "and, believe me, there is something charming in the sound." The quote was later reprinted in Virginia newspapers, and Washington was called the colony's first war hero.

The French did not see him as a hero. Ten Frenchmen were killed and the rest were taken prisoner. Washington watched in shock as the Half-King's warriors scalped the dead. The French prisoners were outraged. They were on a diplomatic mission. Washington had ambushed a peaceful mission and murdered an ambassador. The prisoners called the battle a massacre.

It's never been clear why Washington attacked the French. Did he believe that the French were on their way to attack him? For the rest of his life, he maintained that the attack was justified, but historians disagree, saying that Washington acted too quickly.

Fort Necessity

The French, who were building a fort at the Forks of the Ohio, sent eight hundred soldiers and four hundred Indians to destroy Washington's army. Washington quickly built a log stockade he named Fort Necessity, but his lack of war experience was clear. Fort Necessity wasn't large enough to hold all of Washington's troops. It was also open to a bluff overhead. The Half-King said that Washington would not listen to advice, and he left with many of Washington's Indian allies.

On July 3, 1754, the French attacked. They were led by the brother of the ambassador who had been killed. Washington's soldiers were unprotected from the gunfire that came from the bluffs above the fort. A heavy rain filled their trenches with water and destroyed most of their gunpowder. The battle dragged on for nine hours.

Washington did not want to surrender, but his position was dire. One-third of his troops had been killed. As darkness fell, the French offered to talk. The day after the attack, on July 4—a date Washington never expected to someday celebrate—he signed the surrender on behalf of the British.

The French at Fort Necessity did not take prisoners and generously allowed Washington's troops to go home, with the agreement that they would not return to the Ohio country for one year. Washington was amazed.

The rest of the terms of surrender would haunt Washington for many years. Washington did not speak French, and his interpreter may have given him a bad translation. The document stated that Washington's troops had assassinated the French ambassador, and the French were acting only to avenge his death. Washington claimed that he did not realize that the word

Indians in the French and Indian War

Seneca Indian Chief "Cornplanter"

France had many more Indian allies than England did before and during the war. French settlers were mostly traders who exchanged items like food, guns, and blankets for furs with the Indians. The English, however, were after Indian land. Regardless, the Indians thought it best to fight on the side of the winner. In the early days of the war—especially after Washington's ridiculous defeat at Fort Necessity—the French looked like they were going to triumph.

"assassin" was in the document, perhaps because of a poor translation and also because the document was soaked from the rain. The French used the assassin admission as **propaganda** against the British.

It was an embarrassing defeat. Outside of Virginia, Washington's reputation was left in ruins. The terms of the surrender labeled the British murderers at a time when they were already on the verge of war with France. For the next seven years, the British would wage war on two continents. In Europe, there was the Seven Years' War, and in America, there was the French and Indian War—and Washington had been there when the first shots had been fired.

Over the next five years, he led British troops and the Virginia militia in expeditions against the French. Washington may not have gone to college, but he was an excellent student of war.

CHAPTER 4

The French and Indian War

My inclinations are strongly bent to arms.

Governor Dinwiddie and the Virginia colony recognized Washington's bravery at Fort Necessity. The British military did not. Still, Washington hoped to be rewarded for his efforts. He wanted to make a career as a professional British officer. Washington was a natural leader of men, and fearless on the battlefield.

He wrote to his brother that he wanted to remain a soldier: "My inclinations are strongly bent to arms." His opportunity came the following March. Washington watched from Mount Vernon as British ships sailed up the Potomac River with cannons, soldiers, and the new commander in chief of English forces in North America, Major General Edward Braddock. He intended to do what Washington failed to do—chase the French from the Ohio Valley.

Braddock needed an aide who understood the wilderness, and Washington still wanted to learn all he could about the military. Washington sat and patiently listened to his mother's concerns about his travel, though she eventually stormed angrily out of the room. Washington signed on to Braddock's force as a volunteer aide. He must have been impressed with the

Major General Edward Braddock was born in Perthshire, Scotland, in 1695.

size of the British fighting force—more than two thousand men, a heavy cannon, horses to pull them, and even more horses and wagons to pull the food and supplies. The line, which carved its own road through the wilderness as it went, stretched out for more than six miles.

Washington was impatient. They would never reach Fort Duquesne, where the French had settled by the Ohio River, before winter. Braddock agreed that a column of twelve hundred troops could move forward at full speed. Washington intended to go with them, but he came down with dysentery and had to remain behind. Still, he had no intention of missing the capture of Fort Duquesne. On July 8, 1755, Washington tied pillows to his saddle to protect himself against discomfort and rode to join Braddock.

Major General Edward Braddock intended to do what Washington failed to—chase the French from the Ohio Valley.

Braddock did not listen when Washington warned him that the Canadian French and the Indians did not fight like the French in Europe. Braddock expected lines of French and English soldiers to march toward each other, firing their rifles from across a field as they did in Europe, but the French and Indians had other ideas about how war should be fought. They attacked from the woods, staying hidden behind trees and rocks.

Courage Under Fire

Hearing shots fired ahead, Braddock and Washington led the main column of soldiers forward. An advance team of British Redcoats raced toward them in retreat. The soldiers had no idea what to do when gunfire rang out from the forest around them.

This cartoon was created by Benjamin Franklin in 1754. Franklin urged the colonists to join together—instead of staying separate, like pieces of the snake—to fight against the French.

British soldiers fell in bloody heaps, but instead of a column of soldiers marching forward, all they saw were trees. Shots came at them from every angle, but the guns disappeared before the British could fire back. The Redcoats huddled together in a clearing and started shooting wildly, sometimes hitting each other instead of the enemy. It was impossible to hear orders over the gunshots. The Indians' war whoops added to the confusion. Smoke from the gunpowder stung their eyes and clouded the air, making it hard to see.

Washington wanted to lead colonial troops into the woods to fight the French, but Braddock refused. He believed that kind of warfare was uncivilized.

The British officers had no idea what to do. They were easy targets on their horses. One by one they went down. Washington's horse was shot dead from under him, so Washington jumped on another. Four musket balls tore through

"Redcoats" was the term Americans gave to British soldiers because of the red coats that were part of their uniform.

Captain Thomas Gage

One of the few British officers to survive the Braddock campaign was Captain Thomas Gage. Twenty years later, Washington would meet him again. Gage would become a commander of the British army that would fight outside of Boston at the beginning of the American Revolution.

his coat. His hat was shot right off his head, his second horse crumpled, and yet he still was not hit.

But Braddock was mortally wounded. He ordered Washington to go back forty miles to get reinforcements. Washington rode through the night, passing dead and dying British soldiers. The French and Indians had stopped their attack at nightfall, but it was so dark that Washington sometimes had to get off his horse and look for the road. He fulfilled his mission, but the reinforcements were too frightened to march. England had lost the battle.

Washington was considered a hero of the Braddock campaign. No one blamed him for the disaster. In fact, Washington was singled out for his courage under fire.

Braddock died three days into the retreat. Washington buried him in the middle of the road. To prevent the Indians from scalping him, troops marched over the grave to even out the ground and hide it.

The British and Americans suffered more than nine hundred casualties, while the French and Indians reported only twenty-three dead. The British moved their troops farther north and left the Ohio wilderness to the French.

The defeat taught Washington an important lesson—the powerful English army could be conquered.

Washington was considered a hero of the Braddock campaign. No one blamed him for the disaster. In fact, Washington was singled out for his courage under fire. As the British left the area, Washington was elected "Colonel of the Virginia Regiment and Commander in Chief of all Virginia forces." He was just twenty-three years old. For the next few years, he patrolled the Virginia frontier, protecting English settlers from Indian attacks. He commanded an elite fighting force, but his task was almost impossible.

Finally, the British planned another attack on Fort Duquesne, led by Brigadier General John Forbes. Washington was famous as America's greatest expert on the wilderness and its warfare, and Forbes, like Braddock before him, needed Washington on his team. Washington took command of an advance brigade.

British forces taking over Fort Duquesne in November 1758. This time, the French retreated.

It was his third attempt to win the fort back from the French.

Once again, Washington found himself directly in the line of fire—this time from his own soldiers. Two groups of his troops stumbled upon each other in the wilderness and fired, believing each other to be the enemy. Washington rode between the two lines, knocking their muskets up with his sword. He later wrote that he was in more danger at that moment than he ever was during the Revolutionary War.

When they finally reached Fort Duquesne in late November 1758, the British found it empty and burning. The French, realizing they were greatly outnumbered, had disappeared down the Ohio. The fort Washington had tried to capture twice before, was finally in English hands. After Fort Duquesne, the British won several pivotal battles, and in 1763 the French had relinquished claim to all territory east of the Mississippi River. Despite the early Indian predictions that favored the French, Britain won the French and Indian War.

A New Wife

The Virginia frontier was now safe, and Washington believed his duty was done. He left military life behind and returned to Mount Vernon. His thoughts had turned to other things, like marrying a pretty and wealthy young widow named Martha Dandridge Custis. To the world she became known as Martha Washington. George always called her by her nickname—Patsy.

George and Martha were married on January 6, 1759, in Martha's Virginia home, which was called the White House. George, Martha, and her two children from a previous marriage moved to Mount Vernon. Washington was ready to settle down to life as a Virginia planter.

CHAPTER 5

Trouble with Taxes

Parliament has no right to put its hands into our pockets without our consent.

When George Washington married Martha Dandridge Custis, he became one of the wealthiest planters in Virginia. "I have quit military life," Washington wrote to a friend, "and shortly shall be fixed at this place [Mount Vernon] with an agreeable partner." He lived a peaceful, happy life as a farmer for the next sixteen years. One of the biggest reasons for Washington's happiness was Martha.

Martha, like George, was born on a Virginia plantation. As a girl, she was taught the basics of reading and writing, but her real education was in the art of how to keep a household. When she was eighteen, Daniel Parke Custis proposed. Daniel was the son of one of the wealthiest men in Virginia. His father apparently didn't like anybody—not even his own children. He refused to allow the marriage. But Martha was more than just pretty and smart; she was spirited. She took it upon herself to visit old Mr. Custis. No one knows what she said to him, but Martha and Daniel were soon married.

They had four children together. Two of them died as babies. The

Martha Wasington's first husband was Daniel Parke Custis, who died when Martha was 26 years old.

Under the laws of the time, Martha Washington had to give up all her money and property to George Washington when she married him.

two that survived were John (Jackie) and Martha (Patsy). Jackie was two and Patsy was less than a year old when their father died suddenly. Unexpectedly, Martha was one of the wealthiest widows in Virginia, and she was only twenty-six years old. Most women at that time relied on male relatives when they were widowed, but not Martha. She took over the management of her husband's plantations.

Martha and George met at a cotillion, or a dance, in Williamsburg. She had her pick of suitors, but she fell in love with the handsome young soldier who had been a hero in the French and Indian War. After they were married, Martha turned her attention to caring for her husband and children. She left the management of her plantations to George. George's life as a farmer included managing Mount Vernon and Martha's three plantations, acting as guardian to Martha's two children, foxhunting, and getting involved in Virginia politics.

In 1759, Washington began serving in the Virginia Assembly, also called the House of Burgesses. He went to Williamsburg on his twenty-seventh birthday to take his seat and was elected to the post for fifteen years straight. He served with other famous Virginians, including Thomas Jefferson and Patrick Henry. One of the many committees that George was on worked to reduce the number of stray hogs!

He also fought for veterans' rights. Land had been pledged to the Virginia officers and soldiers who fought by George's side in the French and Indian War. George worked to make sure they received what they had been promised.

Adding land to his own estate was also important to George. He bought land in the Wild West of Virginia as well as land that bordered on Mount Vernon. He more than doubled the size of the plantation. He also doubled the number of slaves he owned. George bought forty-six slaves to work his new land.

Life at Mount Vernon

Just before his marriage, he had built another story to the Mount Vernon house. After the wedding, he made it even bigger—eventually adding two new wings and a two-story parlor. George was his own architect

Like George Washington, Thomas Jefferson was born and raised in Virginia.

George Washington, Stepfather

Although George and Martha never had children of their own, George was much more than a guardian to Martha's children from her first marriage. Patsy was just two years old, and Jackie was four when their mother remarried.

Martha "Patsy" Parke Custis

Before the **boycotts**, the orders George sent to England every year always listed toys and clothes for the children. As a little girl, Patsy started to have seizures. Soon, she was having weekly epileptic fits. No matter what the doctors did, nothing worked. The seizures grew more and more frequent. Patsy died suddenly in 1773 at the age of seventeen. George wrote that it was "a sudden and unexpected blow."

George wanted Jackie to have the kind of education he had missed. But Jackie was spoiled by his mother, and his tutors said he was lazy. He lasted only a few months at King's College and later failed at managing his own plantation. Still, George supported his stepson and even had Jackie join him as an aide at the Battle of Yorktown. Jackie witnessed the British surrender, but soon came down with camp fever. George was at Jackie's bedside when he died two weeks later.

John "Jackie" Parke Custis

and oversaw every detail of the house—even the wallpaper.

Martha enjoyed the social life at Mount Vernon. Many friends lived nearby, including George and Sally Fairfax. The Washingtons liked to entertain, and Martha's family members were among their many visitors. There was always lively conversation around their dinner table.

Mount Vernon was more like a collection of farms than a big plantation. The main cash crop was tobacco. But George saw early on that tobacco robbed the land of its nutrients. He studied agriculture and did experiments, including planting different grains with different fertilizers to see how the plants grew. He even invented a plow that dropped seeds in the furrows.

Eventually, he stopped growing tobacco and planted wheat and corn instead. He built a mill to grind his own wheat into flour, and a schooner to harvest fish from the Potomac. Next came a spinning and weaving business to produce fabric for workers' clothing.

Mount Vernon was more like a collection of farms than a big plantation. The main cash crop was tobacco.

George was determined to turn Mount Vernon into one of the most profitable plantations in Virginia. Unlike his neighbors, he no longer had to depend upon British merchants to sell his tobacco in Europe. He sold his wheat, corn, and fish in Virginia and in the surrounding colonies.

When he stopped growing tobacco, it was as if George declared his independence from British merchants. More and more, the colonists found themselves wondering how much power the British government should have over their lives. This came at a time when leaders in Great Britain began to think of the colonies in a different way.

Even though England had won the French and Indian War against the French, it was a costly victory. England was broke. King George II had died and was succeeded by his grandson, King George III. George III and the British Parliament decided that the colonies should help pay for the war debt and the continued defense of the colonies.

They taxed the colonies.

No Taxation Without Representation

The British Parliament first tried to tax the colonies directly in 1764, when they passed the Sugar Act. Colonists were suddenly forced to pay a tax on molasses imported from the West Indies. Americans protested, but the British Parliament ignored them. The next year, it passed another act—one that would tax much more than molasses.

It took six weeks by sailing ship for news of the Stamp Act of 1765 to reach the colonies. Under the new act, taxed items had to carry a stamp paid for by the buyer. Almost every kind of printed material was taxed, including newspapers, legal documents, and even playing cards.

The Virginia legislature sent a petition to London denouncing the taxes. Other colonies did the same. Americans did not object to paying taxes to their own local governments, but they believed that England had no right to tax them—especially since they were not allowed to vote in Parliament.

The British Parliament, like the American Congress today, established laws that governed the colonies. But the colonists had no representatives in Parliament. "No Taxation Without Representation" became a rallying cry. There was a boycott throughout the colonies. Americans refused to buy English

New Yorkers were not happy about the Stamp Act. They burned stamps in protest.

goods. London merchants suffered. Parliament was forced to repeal, or cancel, the taxes.

George Washington quietly supported the boycotts but didn't join in the public debates. A year later, another wave of

King George III

King George III, the grandson of King George II, was just twenty-two years old when his grandfather died and he became king. He was the first English king in many years who was determined to be more than a figurehead. He intended to rule Great Britain and take back powers that previous kings had passed on to Parliament. But George III wasn't mature enough or self-confident enough to rule his empire. He hired and fired a series of advisers before he brought in Lord Frederick North as prime minister. North was responsible for many of the policies that the American colonists hated.

The more the American colonies resisted British rule, the more determined George III was to hold on to them. He kept up British involvement in the French and Indian War long after many Parliament members wanted it to end. Eventually, North was forced to resign. The British government was in such a shambles after the war that George III considered leaving the throne. Eventually, he found a strong prime minister who was able to restore prosperity and optimism in England.

George III suffered from a form of dementia that may have been caused by a physical illness. At times, his derangement was so bad that others ruled the country in his place. His son, George IV, took over the throne for good in 1811. King George III died in 1820.

taxes was issued by Parliament. Colonists were forced to pay taxes on all goods manufactured in England. "Parliament has no right to put its hands into our pockets without our consent," Washington wrote.

Once again, Americans refused to buy British goods. Finding American substitutes for things like cloth, thread, pins, needles, wallpaper, and even windowpanes wasn't easy for people who bought all their goods from England. Martha trained and oversaw Mount Vernon's spinners, seamstresses, and knitters. George hired weavers to turn the spun flax and thread into fabric.

A Return to Politics

More and more colonists began to speak of liberty—not just from English goods, but from England itself. The British responded by sending four thousand troops to Boston where a group known as the Sons of Liberty had led protests against taxation.

George had been proud to be English. But the more that England refused to listen to the colonists, the angrier he became. On May 18, 1769, he presented a proposal to the House of Burgesses calling for another colony-wide boycott of English goods. With that move, he became a leader in the resistance movement in Virginia. He hoped that England would come to its senses and the colonies could be loyal British subjects once again.

Britain was again forced to **repeal** its taxes. It left one in place, just to make sure that Americans knew who was boss. It was a tax on tea.

CHAPTER 6

The Coming Revolution

I will raise one thousand men, subsist them at my own expense, and march myself at their head for the relief of Boston.

Colonists worked their way around the tea tax by smuggling tea from Holland, and things were quiet for the next few years. Then, in May 1773, Parliament passed the Tea Act, which suddenly made English tea cheaper than smuggled Dutch tea. But if the colonists bought English tea, they would have to pay the British tax.

Colonists wondered if tea was first, what would be next?

Most colonies protested the Tea Act by storing the English tea unsold or by sending it back to Great Britain. But not Massachusetts. In November 1773, the Sons of Liberty prevented three British ships from unloading their cargo of 342 chests of tea. The Royal Governor of Massachusetts, Thomas Hutchinson, would not let the tea ships return to England until the colonists had paid the tax.

Cartoons, such as this skull and crossbones, were printed by colonists to protest the Stamp Act of 1765.

Trouble with Tea

The Sons of Liberty sent a message to Parliament and the governor. It was called the Boston Tea Party.

On the evening of December 16, 1773, about fifty Sons of Liberty painted their faces and disguised themselves as Mohawk Indians. They boarded the three ships and shoveled the tea into the moonlit Boston harbor. In three hours, the tea was completely destroyed. Nothing else on the ships was touched.

When news of the Boston Tea Party reached Britain, the Parliament and the king sent more soldiers to rule over the city and passed new laws to punish Massachusetts. They were angry and embarrassed that a group of colonists had managed to cause so much trouble. Navy ships were sent to close the port of Boston, making it impossible for food and other goods to arrive by sea. Town meetings were outlawed, and colonists were forced to let British soldiers live in their homes. Colonists called these new laws the Intolerable Acts.

To make sure the colonists really got the message, King George III appointed a military leader, General Thomas Gage, to be the new governor of Massachusetts. Gage, an officer who had

The Boston Tea Party

News of the Boston Tea Party reached Washington in the early days of 1774. He disapproved of the Sons of Liberty. Lawless acts would give the British more excuses for an even tighter control over the colonists. But the British retailiation, known as the Intolerable Acts, convinced Washington that something more confrontational than a boycott needed to be done.

The Boston Tea Party

survived Braddock's defeat with George Washington in the French and Indian War, was the commander in chief of the British army in America.

Americans were worried. An attack on liberty in one colony was an attack on them all. They knew that without a port, the people of Boston were in trouble. North Carolina sent food, Connecticut gave hundreds of sheep for milk, wool, and meat, and Virginia sent bushels of corn and wheat.

Washington was shocked by England's response. The king had taken away rights from the people in Boston that all colonists deserved under English law. On Sunday, May 29, 1774, he and other members of the House of Burgesses suggested that men from each colony meet every year to discuss their rights. Two months later, Washington was one of the **delegates** chosen to represent Virginia at the first **Continental Congress**.

The First Continental Congress

Fifty-five delegates from twelve colonies (Georgia did not attend) met in Philadelphia for the first Continental Congress in September 1774. Delegates were chosen or elected by their state

The Shot Heard 'Round the World

Paul Revere planned a warning system to determine how the British troops were approaching. He asked a friend to hang one lantern in the tower of the Old North Church if the British were coming by land, and two lanterns to signal if the troops were coming by sea. Two lanterns shone on April 18, 1775. Revere pounded through the moonlit night on horseback to Lexington to warn the minutemen. The minutemen, a Massachusetts militia, were ready to act "on a minute's warning." After alerting them, Revere rode on to Concord, but he was captured by the British. They put a gun to his head and ordered him to tell the truth. But Revere told some whoppers. He exaggerated the size of the American forces waiting for the British in Concord and claimed that another group of British soldiers had gotten stuck in Boston Bay and would not show up anytime soon. The British took Revere's horse, but they let the brave American go.

In Lexington, seventy-seven minutemen met the British army. The British tried to march past, but a shot rang out. By the time the shooting stopped, eight minutemen had been killed. No one knows who started the skirmish, but the phrase "the shot heard 'round the world" refers to the shots fired at that encounter in Lexington.

The news of the shooting spread to Concord before the British arrived. The Concord minutemen were ready. They took up positions behind barns, houses, walls, and trees. The English soldiers didn't know how to fight an enemy that was hiding. By the end of the day, the British were forced to retreat to Boston.

The American Revolution had begun.

governments. Most were wealthy landowners and businessmen who led the boycotts and protests in their colonies. The men quickly divided into two groups. Some insisted that the colonies needed to immediately declare independence and go to war to defend their liberty. Others argued that a peaceful solution was possible.

At the official sessions of Congress, Washington was mostly silent. He wasn't a public speaker, but Washington loved good company. Over dinners and at tavern meetings with other delegates, he made his views known. He felt it was his duty as a free American to protest the Intolerable Acts. He wasn't ready to call for a break with England, but he was ready to come to the aid of his fellow colonists in Boston. John Adams wrote in his diary, "Colonel Washington says, 'I will raise one thousand men, subsist them at my own expense, and march myself at their head for the relief of Boston.'" After days of debate, with arguments heard from both sides, Congress voted to stop all trade with England. They did not declare independence, but many believed

This scene depicts the skirmish at Lexington between British soldiers and Colonial minutemen that initiated the American Revolution.

war was coming, whether they wanted it or not.

Back in Virginia, Washington began to see that declaring independence was necessary. The Intolerable Acts had pushed many colonists—including Washington—over the line. The British had gone too far. They had to be stopped. And that meant war. Mount Vernon became the headquarters for planning Virginia's response to the crisis in Boston.

Martha watched her husband become one of the leaders of the colonies, and she supported him. The two discussed everything, and she stood firmly on the colonists' side in the split with Great Britain.

A Declaration of Independence

By the time Washington attended the Second Continental Congress in May 1775, fighting had broken out in Lexington and Concord in Massachusetts. The Boston port was crowded with British ships. Soldiers ruled the city, and a small patriot army was in place around Boston. Washington attended Congress in his military uniform. It was his quiet way of supporting the call for independence.

At the Second Continental Congress, some representatives argued for a declaration of independence. Others still hoped to reach a peaceful agreement with England. The delegates agreed on one thing. Boston had been taken over by the British military. Americans had been killed in Lexington and Concord, and the colonies had to defend themselves.

The colonial militia forces surrounding Boston was made up mostly of New

John Adams would become the second U.S. president in 1796.

Englanders. John Adams believed that a commander from a southern colony was the key to making sure that the South joined the fight. Once again, there seemed to be just one man with the skill and experience to do the job: George Washington. Every one of the delegates knew that Washington had been a war hero. He had more military experience than anyone in Congress. And he understood the British military.

The rattlesnake on this flag, known as the Gadsden flag, symbolized colonial defiance and freedom.

When John Adams nominated Washington for the post, Washington left the room so the delegates could debate. The next day, the vote was unanimous. Washington was named commander in chief of the Continental army. Washington accepted his duty to his country, but he did not believe he was up to the difficult task before him. In a speech to Congress, he promised to serve without pay. He added, "I do not think myself equal to the command I am honored with."

Washington was troubled by his doubts, and three days later he wrote to Martha about it. "My Dearest: I am now set down to write you on a subject which fills me with inexpressible concern, and this concern is greatly aggravated and increased when I reflect upon the uneasiness I know it will give you."

He also wrote to Patrick Henry about his worry: "From the day I enter upon the command of the American armies, I date my fall, and the ruin of my reputation."

On June 23, 1775, while Congress continued its debate about independence, Washington set out to join his army.

Chapter 7

First in War

Good God, what brave fellows I must this day lose!

Washington took charge of sixteen thousand militia men outside of Boston on July 3, 1775. It was the twenty-first anniversary of his defeat at Fort Necessity against the French. This time, he would not surrender. His country depended on him. Washington was determined to lead it to victory.

But instead of a fighting force, Washington found a ragtag bunch of soldiers with no sense of order. They were farmers, woodsmen, and clerks dressed in homemade uniforms. Soldiers often ran away—especially just before battle.

Their muskets needed gunpowder to shoot bullets, and there was almost no gunpowder at the camp. When Washington learned that the army had only thirty-six barrels, he was speechless for half an hour. He needed at least four times that much. The army would be helpless to shoot back if the British attacked. Washington sent a messenger into Boston to spread the rumor that they had so much gunpowder—eighteen thousand barrels—that he didn't know what to

Continental soldiers were often not well trained.

The Changing Size of the Army

The size of Washington's fighting force was constantly changing. Most men enlisted in the Continental army for a period of one year—from January 1 to December 31—and went home as soon as their contracts were up. Recruiting became more difficult every year. The army was supposed to include state and local militias—part-time soldiers who would fight when necessary.

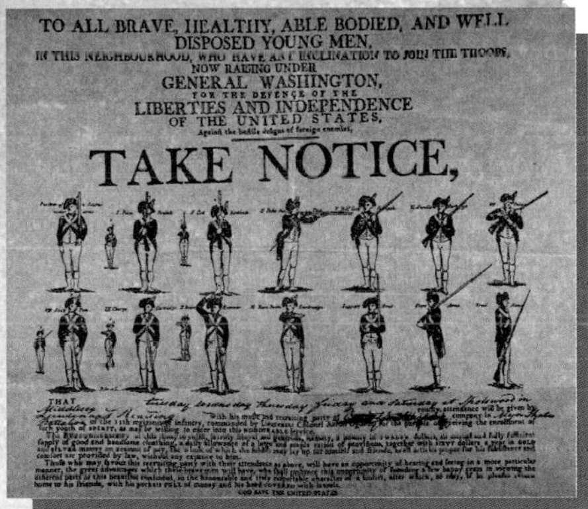

But militias did not always respond when Washington called for help. Often he was forced to send large numbers of his best troops to various areas of the country under the command of his generals to fight other battles. The number of soldiers at the ready was also affected by illnesses like smallpox.

do with it all. The British believed the lie. Washington was able to quietly send appeals for gunpowder across the colonies.

Lack of gunpowder wasn't Washington's only problem. He had to build an army of soldiers from thirteen different colonies that were more like thirteen different countries. The troops did not like discipline, did not follow orders, and didn't trust men from other colonies. Washington was forced to ask himself, Are these the men with which I am to defend America?

He had hoped to spend part of the winter at Mount Vernon, but he was afraid the army would fall apart without him. He wrote to his "Patsy" to ask her to join him in Massachusetts. Martha hated to travel, but that winter—and in all the winters of the war—she joined her husband at his winter camp. The trip from Mount Vernon took almost a month.

The officers and their wives became a happy circle with Martha at the center. But her husband continued to worry about the mistrust among the troops. One day, two different militias got into a snowball fight. Soon, one thousand soldiers were punching and kicking one another. Officers rushed to Washington for help.

Washington leaped on his horse and galloped to the riot. It was the soldiers' first view of Washington's temper. He jumped his horse over a fence and landed right in the middle of the fight. Grabbing two soldiers by their collars, Washington lifted them off the ground—one in each hand—while he roared commands at the others. The fight was over in seconds.

Washington's small army was never as disciplined as the British army, but it was able to keep more than ten thousand British soldiers bottled up in Boston for the next nine months. Washington looked

COMMON SENSE;
ADDRESSED TO THE
INHABITANTS
OF
AMERICA,
On the following interesting
SUBJECTS.

I. Of the Origin and Design of Government in general, with concise Remarks on the English Constitution.
II. Of Monarchy and Hereditary Succession.
III. Thoughts on the present State of American Affairs.
IV. Of the present Ability of America, with some miscellaneous Reflections.

Man knows no Master save creating Heaven,
Or those whom choice and common good ordain.
THOMSON.

PHILADELPHIA;
Printed, and Sold, by R. BELL, in Third-Street.
MDCCLXXVI.

Writer Thomas Paine put all the colonists' criticisms and complaints against British rule into one pamphlet, *Common Sense*, published January 10, 1776.

for a way to fight a battle that would drive the British from the city and end the war. His staff argued that the army wasn't ready, and they were right.

Washington raised the Grand Union flag more than a year before Congress made the Stars and Stripes the official U.S. flag.

Washington was able to send a powerful signal to the British. On January 2, 1776, he celebrated the New Year by raising a new flag on a seventy-six foot schooner mast on Prospect Hill, overlooking Boston. The flag had thirteen red and white stripes—a symbol of the Sons of Liberty—for the thirteen united colonies. The British Union Jack was in the upper left-hand corner. It was a sign that the colonies hoped for justice from King George III. British troops thought it was a flag of surrender and cheered when they saw it. They soon learned otherwise. More than a year would pass before Congress had time to think about an official United States flag. Washington's Grand Union flag saw some of the fiercest fighting in the war.

Redcoats in Retreat

The siege of Boston had become one long staring match. Finally, on the night of March 4, Washington sent three thousand men to Dorchester Heights overlooking Boston to build a series of forts. The British woke up the next morning to find cannons aimed at them from six forts. They had two choices—to attack or to retreat.

An attack was delayed by a powerful storm. General William Howe, who had replaced Thomas Gage, ordered his soldiers to load the Royal Navy's ships as soon as possible. More than one

IN CONGRESS, JULY 4, 1776.

The unanimous Declaration of the thirteen united States of America,

In the Declaration of Independence, Thomas Jefferson outlined the rights Americans desired.

thousand people in Boston who were loyal to King George (called **Tories**) begged Howe to take them with him. Others pleaded with Washington not to fire on the city and destroy their homes. Washington kept his big guns silent while the British worked to load their ships.

On Sunday morning, March 17, small boys raced into Washington's camp to tell him "the lobsters"—their name for the British Redcoats—had left the city. The siege of Boston was finally over. The British sailed for Canada, but Washington knew they would soon invade New York, because the New York harbor was the most important strategic location in the colonies. Not only was it on the coastline, roughly in the middle of the country, but the Hudson River provided easy access to the New England colonies.

As Congress debated whether the colonies should declare independence in the spring of 1776, Washington led his army south to New York City. At the same time, a British fleet carrying thirty-three thousand Redcoats crossed the Atlantic Ocean, sailing closer and closer to the American coastline. They had three hundred supply ships, thirty battleships, and twelve hundred cannons. It was to be the largest seaborne attack England would attempt until World War Two.

In June 1776, while Thomas Jefferson was drafting the Declaration of Independence, Washington was moving fifteen thousand troops into positions on Long Island and Manhattan. In early July, British troops swarmed onto Staten Island.

On July 6, Washington received a copy of the Declaration and sat on horseback while one of his aides read it to his cheering men. They were now citizens of a new country. There was no turning back.

A crowd in New York City, inspired by the Declaration, toppled a lead statue of King George III. One man sawed off the king's head. The rest of the statue was dragged to Connecticut, where it was melted into forty-two thousand musket balls for the Revolutionary army.

Having just heard the Declaration of Independence read aloud for the first time, colonists—inflamed with desire for independence—destroyed a statue of King George III.

Smallpox

More American soldiers died of smallpox than from British bullets. In Boston and New York, as many as a quarter of Washington's soldiers were unfit for duty. Washington was immune because he had survived smallpox as a young man.

Washington kept smallpox patients separate from the rest of the army. He also believed strongly in inoculation against the disease, even though many people at the time thought that inoculation would kill them. In March 1777, Washington made inoculation mandatory for all troops and set up special hospitals to make sure the soldiers were vaccinated. Some historians believe that that policy was the most important strategic decision of Washington's military career.

But the army needed more than musket balls. The Americans were outnumbered and exhausted. By August, they had built more than thirteen forts in New York City, and half a dozen more north of the city. Almost a quarter of Washington's troops were sick with smallpox and camp fever. In his orders on August 20, Washington warned his men that "the army may expect an attack as soon as the wind and tide are favorable."

He was right. British warships moved up the harbor. By noon on August 22, fifteen thousand British troops were on Long Island. Long Island was lost in a day. The British slaughtered the retreating soldiers.

Most of Washington's troops were on Brooklyn Heights. They were protected by thick woods, steep hills, and eight forts with twenty-nine cannons. They were sure they would win any battle with the British.

Surrender or Flee

On August 27, the British began their attack. Unfortunately, they knew more about local geography than Washington did. Loyalists from nearby Queens had shown the Redcoats four passes running through or around Brooklyn Heights. The Americans outside the forts were in danger of attack. They had to surrender or flee.

A bone-chilling rain fell on the battlefield. In some of the American trenches, water rose to the men's waists. Fog clouded their vision, and the British seemed to be everywhere. American soldiers struggled to keep their gunpowder dry. Others gave up and threw away their guns.

Washington was stunned. The Battle of Brooklyn Heights was a disaster for his army. He watched from a fort as a group of brave Maryland soldiers tried to hold back the Redcoats so others could reach an American fort through a marshy canal. The British army stood between the men and the fort. British bullets showered them like hail. The enemy's firepower was overwhelming. Still the Marylanders advanced on the British not once but four times. "Good God, what brave fellows I must this day lose!" Washington shouted. Deaths numbered 259, and about another hundred were wounded. The few men who survived crawled out of a mucky creek, looking like water rats.

These two musket balls were used as bullets. These particular ones were also given to patients to bite on during surgery—an especially painful experience in Colonial times due to the lack of anesthesia.

Inside the fort, the Continental army was trapped. Washington knew that if he did not retreat, the war would be lost. The only way out was by water—across the East

River from Brooklyn into Manhattan. He sent orders to New York City to collect every boat that would float. At midnight on August 29, under the cover of rain and fog, the retreat began.

For awhile the retreat went smoothly. Then a strong wind blew in the wrong direction, making the use of sailboats impossible. Only rowboats could be used. An aide told Washington there was no hope of getting all the men to New York by morning.

Suddenly the wind shifted and the water became as smooth as glass. When morning approached, an even thicker fog settled in, protecting the Americans from British eyes. The haze remained until all the soldiers escaped. By the time Washington stepped onto the last boat, he had not closed his eyes for two whole days.

When the fog finally cleared, the British were amazed. The Americans were gone! Washington had outfoxed them, and his men lived to fight another day.

For the next three months, Washington kept his troops on the northern edge of Manhattan. In November, the British captured Fort Washington and Fort Lee in a defeat that was even worse than the one at Brooklyn Heights. Almost three thousand Americans were killed or captured. Most of the army's cannons

"His Excellency"

George Washington received letters of congratulations from the New York and the Massachusetts legislatures. Both were addressed to "His Excellency." From then until the end of the war, Washington was known as "His Excellency."

George Washington leading the retreat from Brooklyn Heights into Manhattan across the East River.

and muskets had to be left behind in the retreat.

Washington's army escaped across the Hudson River and New Jersey. Early in December, the frozen and hungry soldiers crossed the Delaware River into Pennsylvania. Congress feared that the British would soon march on Philadelphia, and Washington's orders were to protect the city. He made sure the British couldn't follow and ordered that all the boats be moved to the Pennsylvania side of the river.

The fate of the United States rested on Washington and six thousand men. By that time, many Americans had stopped supporting the war. Even Washington had considered leaving the army. "It seems impossible to continue my command in this situation," he wrote, "but if I withdraw, all will be lost."

There were many dark moments in the war. This was one of the darkest. Washington never lost faith in himself and his brave soldiers, but he knew that the support of Congress and the American people were necessary to win the war.

Washington needed a victory—and soon.

CHAPTER 8

Victory or Death

Away my dear Colonel, and bring up the troops. The day is ours.

The Continental army was in desperate need of a victory before the end of the year, when many of Washington's soldiers were scheduled to go home. He had called on New Jersey's sixteen thousand militia men to join him, but only one thousand men responded.

General William Howe withdrew the British troops to Manhattan and Staten Island for the winter, leaving small military posts in New Jersey. The post nearest to Washington's troops in Trenton, just across the Delaware River, was manned by Hessian soldiers from Germany. The Hessians were professional soldiers hired by the British.

Washington decided to attack with the kind of hit-and-run raids he saw the Indians use in the French

Many German soldiers came from the German state called Hesse, which is how they got their name, "Hessians."

Washington Crossing the Delaware was painted by German-born Emanuel Leutze in 1851.

and Indian War. It was a daring and unexpected plan, scheduled for Christmas Day.

Twenty-four hundred soldiers from the Continental army marched under the cover of darkness and boarded large cargo boats. The night was bitter cold and chunks of ice rushed by in the current of the Delaware River, threatening to smash the boats to pieces.

The army was in no shape to stage an attack. The men had little food and almost no warm clothes. Their shoes had simply fallen off their feet as the soldiers marched in retreat across New Jersey.

A Desperate March

As the troops reached the far shore, a storm broke. The little army split into two columns. It was a desperate nine-mile march. The road was a sheet of ice beneath the men's bloody feet. The wind beat sleet and hail into the soldiers' backs. If a man sat down to rest, he might never get up again.

Washington leading his men during the daring raid on Trenton

Washington rode up and down the two columns, urging his officers to remind their men of their password: "Victory or Death."

The sleet soaked through the men's gunpowder. A quick check revealed that almost none of the guns would fire. An officer asked Washington what he should do. "Use the bayonet," Washington said. "The town must be taken."

There were rumors of an American attack, but the Germans never expected it to come on Christmas Day. They were either sleeping or were too exhausted to stand guard. They were taken completely by surprise.

The Americans had ducked into houses to dry their gunpowder. They positioned themselves and shot from windows and doorways. The Germans were blinded by the snow. They couldn't see where the shots were coming from. Surrender came quickly. The Battle of Trenton turned out to be Washington's most brilliant war effort. The Continental army was on the offensive for the first time. Washington learned a valuable lesson: His army could not overcome the powerful enemy head-on, but it could win small, well-planned attacks.

But the British weren't about to let Washington get away with it again. Lord Charles Cornwallis, a general in the British army, led a column of more than fifty-five hundred men toward Washington, ready for revenge.

The American soldiers were holed up behind a small river on the western edge of Trenton. When the British arrived in the late afternoon, they set up tents on the other side of the river. Cornwallis was sure that he could defeat Washington in the morning.

As soon as darkness fell, Washington sent his supplies south. American officers ordered their soldiers to build their campfires higher than usual. Then, one by one, the American regiments quietly marched away. A few men stayed behind to keep the fires burning during the night.

The British woke up the next morning to discover that Washington's troops had disappeared. Washington had outfoxed them yet again!

A Second Victory

Overnight, Washington marched toward the village of Princeton. Cornwallis had left behind twelve hundred men in the British camp at Princeton. The battle began as Washington galloped ahead of his soldiers in an advance against the British.

After the American Revolution, General Charles Cornwallis was made governor-general of India, where he died in 1805.

He was such an obvious target on his big horse that an aide was sure Washington would get killed. The aide covered his face with a hat so he wouldn't have to watch. When the smoke cleared, Washington was still on his horse. "Away, my dear Colonel, and bring up the troops," Washington said. "The day is ours."

The British were on the run. Washington joined the chase and they surrendered. Before leaving Princeton with between two and three hundred prisoners, Washington set fire to the enemy's gunpowder. Suddenly, instead of occupying New Jersey, the British controlled barely one-fifth of it. Everywhere else, the new American government was in charge.

Many citizens of New Jersey had sworn their loyalty to the British as the Redcoats marched through. Washington's officers wanted to see these traitors punished. But Washington knew that many of them claimed loyalty to the king because they were afraid. Instead of punishing them, Washington proposed that they be allowed to pledge **allegiance** to the United States. Those who refused to do so, were permitted to bring with them any possessions that would not aid the enemy and then marched unharmed to the enemy lines.

Having to choose between Washington's kindness and the spite of the British military, many Tories decided to become patriots.

Washington knew that the fastest way to turn a Tory into an American patriot was to send him to British-controlled New York. The British military treated colonists badly. Having to choose between Washington's kindness and the spite of the British military, many Tories decided to become patriots.

The victories at Trenton and Princeton did not inflict serious damage on the British, but they had a huge effect on American

Tories faced taunting, ridicule, and sometimes violence and imprisonment. Many moved to Canada and England during the Revolution.

public opinion. After a long string of defeats and surrenders, Washington's army had put the British on the run. Americans started to believe that they could win the war. Nearly half of Washington's army agreed to stay on for another year.

From then on, Washington realized that the way to win the war was to hold his troops together and outlast the British. He spent the rest of the winter organizing his army. During the spring, there were a few small battles. That summer, the British marched on Philadelphia, the capital, with reinforcements of seven thousand men from across the ocean. The Continental Congress ordered Washington to defend the capital and then it moved again—this time to York, Pennsylvania.

Defending Philadelphia

War was advancing on two fronts. British General John Burgoyne was traveling south from Canada while General Howe set sail from New York for Philadelphia. Congress sent Horatio Gates, a popular general, to lead the New England militias

A Small Victory

Men often brought their dogs to war in colonial times. Two days after the Battle of Germantown, General Howe's dog was found wandering behind American lines. Washington, always a gentleman, returned the dog to General Howe with a note: "General Washington's compliments to General Howe. He does himself the pleasure to return him a dog, which accidentally fell into his hands, and by the inscription on the collar appears to belong to General Howe."

against Burgoyne. Washington led the Continental army south to defend Philadelphia.

Washington's army faced Howe's troops on September 11, 1777, at the Battle of Brandywine Creek. The Americans fought bravely, but they were outnumbered. Howe took Philadelphia on September 26.

Washington retreated and planned another surprise attack at Germantown, Pennsylvania, on October 3. At the onset of the Germantown battle, the American troops were getting the better of the British. Then everything suddenly changed. Washington's front lines had run out of ammunition and started to retreat. Another column of American soldiers ran into them. The confused troops fired on each other in the dense fog and smoke. By the end of the battle, the British held the field. American casualties were double the number of those on the British side.

General Howe must have been impressed with the improvement of the Americans' military skill at Germantown, even though the British had won the battle. Howe started to take the Continental army more seriously and made sure the

Americans couldn't wage any more surprise attacks. He withdrew the entire British fighting force behind fortifications that he had built in Philadelphia.

The losses at Germantown were hard on Washington's troops. Fortunately, farther north, the Americans defeated the British and General Burgoyne at the Second Battle of Saratoga. In this second attack, the Continental army was led by on of its most heroic fighters, Benedict Arnold. The American victory sent shock waves as far away as London and Paris. The British considered getting out of the war. And the French considered getting in—on the side of the Americans.

But it was too soon to know that. Washington led his tired troops to their 1777–1778 winter quarters at Valley Forge, Pennsylvania. It was a long, sad march without coats or shoes in the terrible cold.

The British surrender at Saratoga boosted the Continental army's confidence.

CHAPTER 9

Valley Forge

Starve—dissolve—or disperse.

Saratoga may have been the turning point for the French to decide to join the war. But for Washington, who struggled with his troops day after day through a long hard winter, the true turning point was Valley Forge.

The British left Washington's troops alone that winter, but they had to battle other enemies—cold and hunger. Congress lacked the power to supply money or food, and state governments were too far away, or unwilling, to support

A desperate night at Valley Forge

the troops. The harvest had been plentiful that year, but many farmers chose to sell to the British in Philadelphia, who had real money to spend.

Washington wrote to the president of the Continental Congress "that unless some great… change [took] place…this Army must inevitably be reduced to one or other of these three things. Starve—dissolve—or disperse."

A Dark, Hungry Winter

The men were forced to live in tents until they could build crude log cabins. Bloody footprints marked the snow from the soldiers' shoeless feet. Their uniforms fell apart. Sometimes it took the clothes of a whole unit to outfit one man who had guard duty in the cold. Most of the horses died of starvation or from the extreme cold. Even water was in short supply.

By the time Martha arrived in February 1778, soldiers were on the verge of starvation. They cheered when she arrived. They had learned to look for her carriage as a sign that the fighting was over until the spring.

Conditions improved and food became more plentiful. Two men arrived at camp that winter. They raised everyone's spirits. One was the Marquis de Lafayette, a

The Marquis de Lafayette forged a lasting friendship with George Washington when he joined the colonists against the British in 1777.

twenty-year-old French nobleman who had been wounded at Brandywine. Lafayette became like a son to Washington and was one of his bravest officers. He was given command of an army division and he shared the soldiers' hardships at Valley Forge—at times spending his own money to buy them warm clothing. His men called him "the soldiers' friend."

The other was Lieutenant General Friedrich Wilhelm Ludolf Gerhard Augustin, Baron von Steuben. His title was totally made up, and Steuben had never really been a general under Frederick the Great like he said, but he was an expert at drilling troops. Like many Europeans who lived under monarchies, Steuben admired the Americans' desire for liberty. Soon after he arrived at camp, Steuben was barking orders to platoons in a mixture of German and French curse words. Drilling with Steuben became the favorite sport at Valley Forge. Companies of soldiers competed with each other to be the best. Steuben raised morale and taught Washington's soldiers the skills they needed to match the British on an open

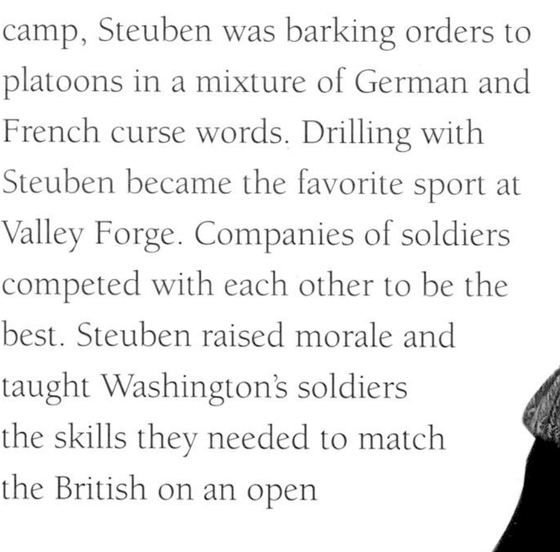

Baron von Steuben not only served as drill instructor, but also set rules for sanitation and cleanliness at camp that helped save soldiers' lives.

battlefield. They became a truly professional army.

But it was still a small army. Many had deserted or left the army at the end of the year when their contracts ran out. Illnesses like smallpox had taken others. Washington made sure that rumors of much higher numbers reached the enemy. The British, who had fifteen thousand troops wintering in nearby Philadelphia, could have ended the war at any time. They believed Washington's rumors and didn't attack.

It was also during that dark, hungry winter at Valley Forge that Washington developed a new kind of leadership. His army was at the point of total collapse. The Continental Congress was powerless to support the soldiers. Still, Washington managed to hold them together. For Washington and his men, the meaning of the American Revolution changed. It became more than a war for independence. When they joined the army, Washington and his troops fought for their own states. Now they banded together to fight for one nation.

When they joined the army, Washington and his troops fought for their own states. Now they banded together to fight for one nation.

A Turn for the Better

Things finally began to take a turn for the better in May 1778. Washington learned that the French were sending ships and troops, and the British were beginning to make plans to leave Philadelphia for New York.

In mid-June, the washerwomen who spied for Washington reported that the British had ordered their laundry at once—clean or dirty. Washington knew that the march to New York was

The Marquis de Lafayette

Marie Joseph Paul Yves Roch Gilbert du Motier, the Marquis de Lafayette, was a French aristocrat who fell in love with the democratic principles of the American cause.

At Washington's request, Congress gave him command of an army division. He was just twenty years old when he joined Washington's staff. Lafayette quickly became close to his commander in chief and proved to be a brilliant and fearless battlefield general.

He went back to France at the end of the war and took a leading role in the early days of the French Revolution. He sent Washington a symbol of the French cause—the key to the Bastille.

about to start. He ordered the Marquis de Lafayette to take five thousand men and strike hard whenever the British looked open to attack. But one of Washington's other officers, Major General Charles Lee, insisted that he be put in charge of the attack instead of Lafayette because he had a higher rank.

Lee's attack was confused and weak. When the British counterattacked, Lee ordered his soldiers to retreat. Washington was furious. He rode into battle and took charge. After months of Steuben's drilling, the army held its own against the more powerful British forces. That night it was the British who slipped away under the cover of darkness. Lee was court-martialed, or summoned by a military court.

Congress returned to Philadelphia on July 2—just in time to celebrate the second anniversary of its independence.

Philadelphia remained in American hands for the rest of the war.

The British spent the rest of 1778 behind their fortifications in New York. Washington's troops faced another long, hard winter in Morristown, New Jersey. As the spring, summer, and autumn of 1779 slowly passed, Washington desperately hoped for French support in pushing the British out of New York. But the French navy was patrolling the West Indies instead of coming to the aid of the Americans.

As Martha did every winter, she arrived to create a warm home for her husband. Still, Washington wrote to Congress that his soldiers ate "every kind of horse food but hay."

Great Britain had considered pulling out of the war after their defeat at Saratoga. But when the French joined the fight on the side of the Americans, King George grew more determined to win. More British soldiers sailed for America, heading south.

Washington spent much of his time trying to get the French to join him in an assault on New York City. At the same time, he petitioned the states for money, supplies, and fresh recruits. The winter of 1779–1780 at Morristown brought the lowest temperatures and the biggest blizzards in memory. Snow drifts were six feet high.

As Martha did every winter, she arrived to create a warm home for her husband. Still, Washington wrote to Congress that his soldiers ate "every kind of horse food but hay." The troops went days without food and months without pay. Whole companies were on the verge of mutiny.

Things seemed to hit bottom. Then, they got even worse. One of Washington's most trusted generals was exposed as a traitor.

Chapter 10

The Long Road to Victory

Arnold has betrayed us! Who can we trust now?

Benedict Arnold was Washington's greatest combat general and one of the biggest heroes of the Revolution. With less than one hundred men, he and Ethan Allen had seized Fort Ticonderoga and captured British guns even before the war had officially begun. He was a courageous leader in later battles, including the victory at Saratoga.

Arnold was recovering from a serious leg wound when Washington named him military commander of Philadelphia after the British left in May 1778. At that time, Arnold married Peggy Shippen, the daughter of a Philadelphia loyalist, and began living a lavish life that he couldn't afford. Many patriots suspected that Arnold could no longer be trusted, since his wife was believed to be on the side of the British.

Washington never doubted his friend. He was glad to see that Arnold had found a wife and hoped that all of Philadelphia's loyalists would join the patriot cause, now that the British had left the city.

Hundreds of years after his fateful act, Benedict Arnold's name is still linked with the word "traitor."

Arnold was charged with taking bribes to support his new lifestyle, and Washington was forced to order a court-martial. Arnold was cleared of all but two minor charges. Washington was pleased that the great soldier was free for more active military duty.

But Arnold was angry, and he had other ideas. Encouraged by his pro-British wife, he offered his services to Peggy's old friend—British army officer John André. Major André urged Arnold to secure command of West Point.

If West Point was captured, the Hudson and all of New England would be open to the British fleet.

West Point was Washington's major fort on the Hudson River. If West Point was captured, the Hudson and all of New England would be open to the British fleet. On August 3, 1780, Washington gave Arnold control of the fort. Washington had no way of knowing that Arnold was preparing to hand it over to the British—in exchange for money and a position in the British army.

Arnold had commanded West Point for two months when Washington decided to visit his good friend and inspect the fort. A few hours before Washington's arrival, Arnold fled downriver to an English warship. He had discovered what Washington did not yet know: Major André had been captured by American forces and he was found to have papers from Arnold hidden in his shoes.

"Arnold has betrayed us!" Washington cried, when he learned the news. "Who can we trust now?" For the rest of the war, Washington was determined to get revenge. He wanted to see Arnold hanged as a spy, but the British refused to give him up—even in exchange for Major André, who was later hanged himself.

Arnold became a general in the British army. The British tried to use his plot to hurt American morale. But such hatred for the traitor spread throughout the states that it strengthened the patriot cause.

The War Moves South

The British sent troops south, but Washington was forced to stay in the New York area to control his own troops—many had threatened mutiny if they were not paid—and contain the British forces in the city. Lafayette and others were sent south with a fighting force.

The British invaded Virginia, and Thomas Jefferson was forced to flee into the mountains. During April 1781, the British sloop, or sailboat, *Savage* sailed up the Potomac and trained her guns on Mount Vernon. Washington's estate manager saved Mount Vernon by supplying the British with food. When Washington learned of it, he wrote an angry letter, saying he would rather "they had burnt my house and laid the plantation in ruins," than aid the enemy.

By the summer of 1781, American

British General John André drew this self-portrait while in prison.

George Washington, Spymaster

George Washington was an expert at making the British believe false information by spreading rumors and planting fake documents on messengers. After Washington decided to march south to Yorktown, he sent engineers to prepare what looked like a major camp in New Jersey—complete with ovens for baking thousands of loaves of bread! The British believed he was preparing to attack New York, and two thousand British soldiers prepared to defend the city. By the time they realized Washington was headed south, it was too late to send reinforcements to Yorktown.

victory seemed impossible. The French had sent troops and ships but refused to join Washington in an attack on New York. His own army couldn't do the job without the help of the French navy.

British troops had taken Savannah, Georgia; and Charleston, South Carolina. The governors of Virginia and South Carolina urged Washington to take his army south. On August 14, Washington learned that a large French fleet had left the West Indies and was finally sailing to America. It was headed for the Chesapeake Bay.

Washington and the French army marched south to meet the French navy.

British General Charles Cornwallis had moved his entire army to Yorktown, Virginia, on the Chesapeake Bay. The Marquis de Lafayette's force blocked the Redcoats' escape route by land. The French fleet arrived and blocked escape by sea.

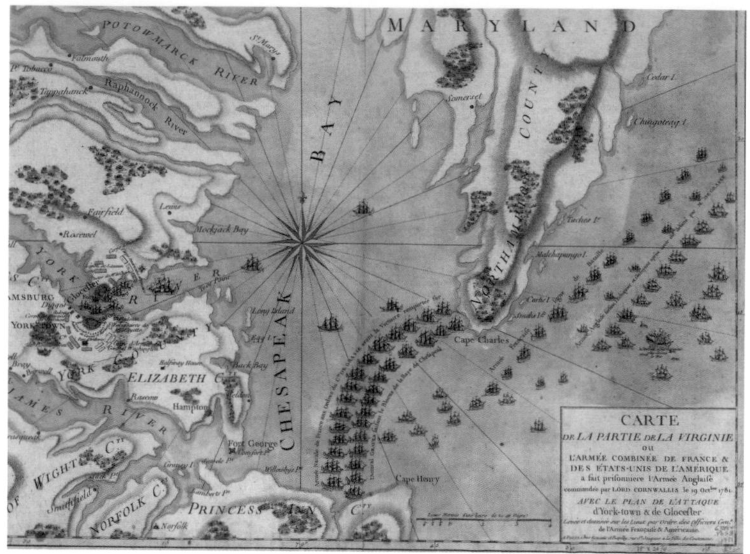

Map of Yorktown

A Final Victory at Yorktown

By the time Washington marched on Yorktown, the British were trapped. On October 9, with trenches dug and cannons positioned, Washington put a match to the first big gun and sent a twenty-four-pound cannonball whistling through Yorktown. American and French forces pounded away at the British day and night, drawing closer and closer.

Cornwallis sent Washington a letter on October 17, asking for a meeting to settle the terms of surrender. Two days later, Washington sat astride Nelson, his favorite horse, while the defeated British troops marched out of Yorktown between the French and American armies.

British General Cornwallis claimed to be too sick to attend the surrender ceremony. His representative, Charles O'Hara, tried to hand his sword to the French general Rochambeau instead of

Washington, but the Frenchman refused. O'Hara had no choice but to surrender his sword to an American.

Washington did not know this would be the last battle of the war, and he was not able to celebrate the victory. His stepson, Jackie Custis, who had joined him at Yorktown as an aide, was sick with "camp fever." Jackie witnessed the surrender but died two weeks later.

After Yorktown, Washington held the army together. He was afraid the British would respond as they had in the past—by sending more troops. But this time, the British agreed to sign a peace treaty and recognize the United States as an independent nation. The Revolutionary War was over.

The British tried to surrender to the French at Yorktown, but they were forced to turn their weapons over to the Americans.

The signing of the Treaty of Paris was to be commemorated by painter Benjamin West. But the British allegedly refused to sit for the painting, so it remains unfinished.

Negotiations for peace dragged on for almost two years. Finally, the Treaty of Paris was signed in September 1783. Two months later, the British army and navy left New York.

Washington and his remaining officers rode into New York City on the day the British departed. As a last insult, the British left their flag flying over Fort George with the ropes cut and the flag pole greased. Washington's victory parade through the city was delayed until a sailor was finally able to climb up the pole and hoist an American flag in its place.

Washington commanded the army in what would be, until the Vietnam War, the longest war in American history. He was forty-three years old when he left Mount Vernon for the Second Continental Congress. When he arrived back home, he was fifty-one. The British had changed commanding officers four times. Washington outlasted them all.

In December, Washington said farewell to his officers at Fraunces Tavern in New York City. With tears streaming down his face, Washington said good-bye to the men who had fought by his side for so many years.

Washington left New York and rode to Annapolis, Maryland, where Congress was meeting. There was a formal dinner and a dance to honor His Excellency on December 22. Ladies lined up in rows to dance with him. The next day, after almost nine years of service to his country, Washington resigned his commission.

Martha stood waiting for him, as he rode up the circular drive to Mount Vernon. It was Christmas Eve 1783. Washington was home at last.

General George Washington says good-bye to his men at Fraunces Tavern in New York City. Fraunces Tavern still stands today.

CHAPTER 11

Private Citizen

We are either a united people, or we are not.

Washington may have longed for a peaceful life at Mount Vernon, but the plantation had been neglected for years and there was much work to be done.

Mount Vernon was huge. It stretched for ten miles along the Potomac and was four miles broad at its widest point. There were five different farms, each with its own overseer, slave workforce, livestock, and buildings. Every

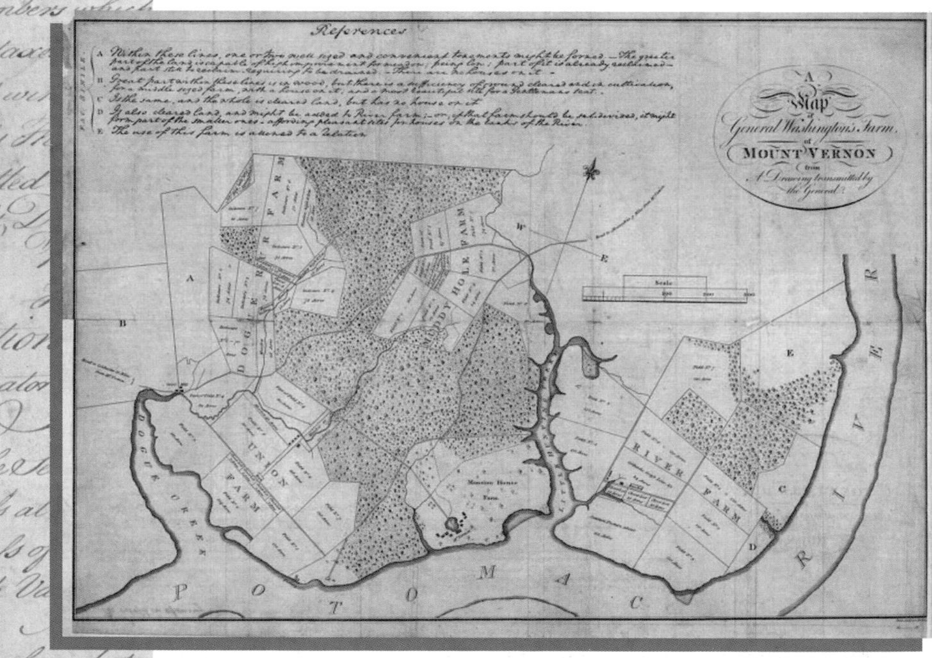

Map of Mount Vernon's five farms

A cross-section of Washington's sixteen-sided barn.

morning except Sunday, Washington rode out and inspected his farms after his seven o'clock breakfast of "three small Indian hoecakes (buttered) and many dishes of tea (without cream)."

Managing a plantation the size of Mount Vernon was like running a small town. In addition to the farms and the field hands, Washington had a staff that included blacksmiths, shoemakers, tailors, gardeners, spinners, and weavers.

As he had in the past, Washington conducted farm experiments. He invented a system of crop rotation and ran a wheat-grinding mill. When the king of Spain and the Marquis de Lafayette both sent donkeys as gifts (named Royal Gift and King of Malta), Washington started another business breeding a first-rate line of mules.

A sixteen-sided barn for wheat thrashing was Washington's most interesting invention. Until then, wheat was thrashed by hand. Thrashing was a long, slow process that involved beating wheat to separate the grain from the straw. Horses could be used to trample the wheat, but that had to be done outside. Dirt and dung got mixed in with the grain.

Washington designed a barn that was big enough to bring the horses indoors. Horses ran in a circle on the barn's second floor to tread the grain out of the wheat. The wheat fell between gaps in the wooden floor planks to a brick floor below. Then it was taken to the mill for grinding.

After the long years of war, there was also work to be done on the mansion house. Washington finished work on the grand dining room. A spacious porch was added to the front of the house—the perfect setting for afternoon tea and a majestic view of the Potomac. He also added a dove of peace weathervane to

George and Martha Washington with their grandchildren, Nelly and Wash Custis. The servant standing behind Martha is thought to be William Lee.

the roof to celebrate the end of the war.

The mansion house was always full of people and lively conversation. George and Martha had adopted Jackie's two youngest children when he died, and became guardians to one of Martha's nieces and a number of George's nieces and nephews.

The Dove of Peace weathervane

Washington himself was the most famous man in America. Friends and strangers came to pay tribute to His Excellency. Martha took care of them all. The nearest inn was several hours away by horseback, so many guests stayed overnight.

A Return to Politics

More and more, discussions at Mount Vernon started to sound like they had in 1775. Politics was the main topic of conversation. The new nation stood on shaky ground. There were thirteen states, but they were not united.

The Articles of Confederation, adopted by the Second

Pen Pals

Congress had passed a law that allowed all letters to or from Washington to be sent free. Washington received so much mail after the war that he couldn't keep up with it. A team of aides was hired to make sure that every single letter was answered.

This woodcut depicts Daniel Shays (left) and Job Shattuck (right) who were both leaders in the Massachusetts rebellion. The image was used on the cover of a pamphlet created to drum up support for Shays's Rebellion.

Continental Congress, were like a partnership agreement that helped the states band together during the war. Now that their common enemy had been defeated, the states acted like thirteen independent countries. They printed their own money and charged one another high taxes when goods were sent from state to state. The British, who violated the peace treaty by keeping troops on the western frontier, made the situation worse by pitting states against each other.

It became clear to Washington that the American Revolution wasn't over. The Continental Congress was powerless, and the United States needed a strong central government if the nation was to survive.

In 1786, the states were forced to agree. Daniel Shays, a former Continental army captain, was about to lose his small

Massachusetts farm. All around him, other farmers were losing their land because they could not pay the taxes or their bills. Shays decided to fight his tax problem the way he had fought in the war. He formed a militia and marched on the state capital.

Shays's Rebellion spread throughout Massachusetts. The governor called on Congress for help, but Congress had no money to raise an army to defend the state. The rebellion ended after one battle, but protests spread to other states. Washington urged his friend James Madison, a member of the Virginia general assembly, to ask the legislature to call for reform. Madison, who would go on to become the fourth president of the United States, had helped write the Virginia constitution. He worked closely with Thomas Jefferson to establish religious freedom as part of Virginia law. Washington knew Madison's voice would be important in calling for a stronger central government.

"We are either a united people, or we are not," Washington wrote to Madison. "If the former, let us, in all matters of general concern act as a nation."

A New Convention

A convention of all states was scheduled to meet in Philadelphia in May 1787 to revise the Articles of Confederation. Washington was elected to lead the Virginia delegation. At first, he refused to go. When he left the army, he said that his public career was over. Also, he hated to leave Mount Vernon. What would Americans think if he went back on his word? Martha agreed. She was much happier at home at Mount Vernon than anywhere else, and she didn't want her husband to get involved in the nation's business again.

Madison, Jefferson, and others convinced Washington to change his mind. The success of the convention depended on his

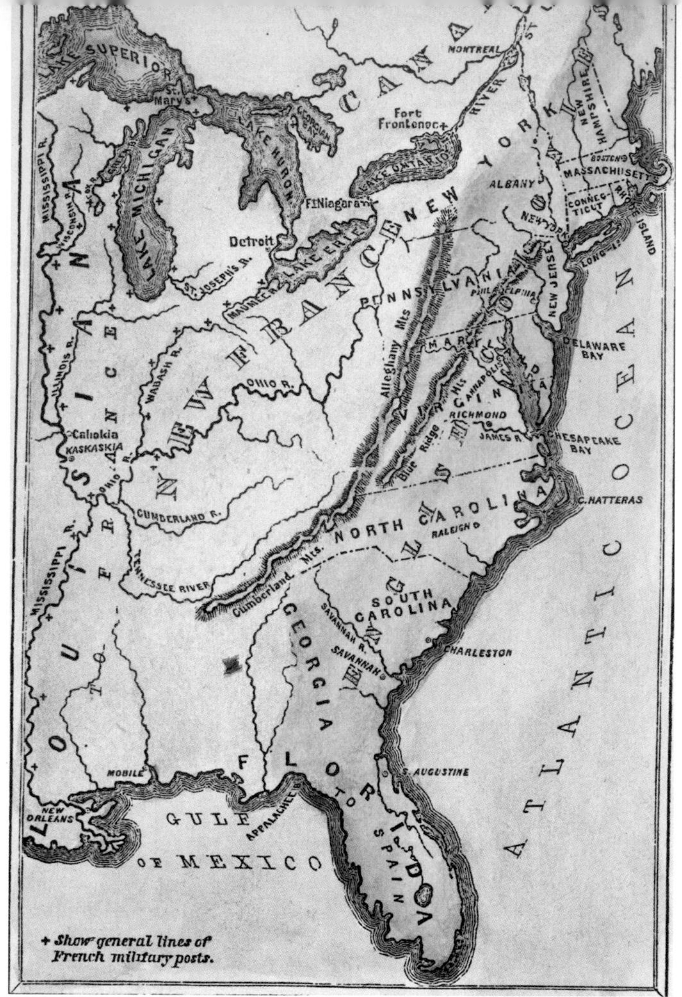

Representatives from twelve of the thirteen states (shown in red) gathered in Philadelphia for the Constitutional Convention.

steady presence. They assured him that afterward he could return to his retirement.

Martha was too busy with the children to go with Washington. It would be lonely in Philadelphia without her, but his country needed him, so he set out on May 9, 1787.

When he arrived in Philadelphia four days later, Washington's first stop was at the house of Benjamin Franklin. Franklin and Washington had been friends since the Second Continental Congress and would serve together at the new Constitutional Convention.

Delegates from twelve states (Rhode Island did not attend) gathered in what we now call Independence Hall in Philadelphia. The first order of business was to elect a president of the convention. Washington was the most famous and trusted man in the nation. The vote was unanimous for Washington.

Washington took a seat at the front of the room, facing the delegates. As president of the convention, he was not allowed to participate in the debates. But his views were well known. He believed in a strong central government. His commanding

Independence Hall in Philadelphia. Delegates debated points in the Constitution for four months.

The Three Branches of Government

The Constitution established a three-part government with a system of checks and balances that prevented any one branch from becoming too powerful and taking away the liberties guaranteed to the people. The three branches are:

1. Executive Branch
The president and vice president of the United States

2. Legislative Branch
The House of Representatives and the Senate

3. Judicial Branch
The Supreme Court and all lower courts

presence at the front of the room was a reminder to the delegates that they had come together to create a strong union.

Within five days, the delegates realized that they had to totally scrap the Articles of Confederation and create a new constitution. Delegates debated for the next four months. The meetings were so secret that windows in some rooms were nailed shut. Oftentimes, it seemed as though the delegates would never reach agreement.

On September 17, at the end of a long, hot summer, delegates voted to accept the draft of the Constitution of the United States and present it to the states for their approval. It was based on a bold new idea. The Constitution put forth a government that was directly responsible to the people.

Nine states had to **ratify**, or approve, the Constitution in order for it to become law. Voters in every state knew that Washington had been the first to sign the document.

Delaware was the first state to ratify the new Constitution, followed by Pennsylvania and New Jersey. Other states did not approve it so quickly. There were passionate debates for and against the Constitution in newspapers, town squares, and state legislatures. People feared that the central government—especially the president—would be too powerful, taking away the rights of state and local governments. Could the president become a king or a dictator? they wondered.

Many people voted for the Constitution only because they knew that Washington would become the first president. He had walked away from power at the end of the war, and Americans trusted that he would take on the role in the new government without abusing his power.

Massachusetts became the next state legislature to vote yea by a narrow margin—187 to 168, followed by Georgia and

Rather than revise the Articles of Confederation, delegates at the Constitutional Convention opted to write a new constitution to govern their new country.

Washington would have rather stayed at Mount Vernon, but his country needed his leadership.

Connecticut. Then, Maryland and South Carolina approved. The Constitution needed to be ratified by just one more state to become law.

From Mount Vernon, Washington tracked the results state by state. He wanted the Constitution ratified, but he was less enthusiastic about what that would mean for him. He knew he would be elected president. Washington believed it was his duty to lead his country once again, but he longed to stay at Mount Vernon and live the life of a retired farmer.

June 1788 became the month of decision. New Hampshire, Virginia, and New York were all meeting to vote on the Constitution. By late June, word came to Mount Vernon that all three states had ratified.

Washington stood on his porch at Mount Vernon. The Potomac was aglow with the lights of boats coming to offer him congratulations. Cannons roared in celebration. Eventually the two hold-out states—North Carolina and Rhode Island—would vote yes as well.

Under the Constitution, electors from each state voted for

the president. The electors were chosen on January 7, 1789, by the vote of the people in some states, and by the legislature in others. On February 4, 1789, the **Electoral College** met to choose the first president of the United States. Once again, the unanimous vote was for Washington.

We the People of the United States, in Order to form a more perfect Union, establish Justice, insure domestic Tranquility, provide for the common defence, promote the general Welfare, and secure the Blessings of Liberty to ourselves and our Posterity, do ordain and establish this Constitution for the United States of America.

Article. I

The Constitution of the United States. George Washington was the first person to sign the finished document.

Chapter 12

First in Peace

I do solemnly swear that I will faithfully execute the office of president of the United States.

Washington began to look forward to the idea of leading such a glorious experiment. If the United States could succeed as a nation, it would prove to the whole world that men could govern themselves without a king or a dictator standing over them.

Washington's bags were packed. He grew worried and impatient as he waited week after week for word from Congress, but the electors' ballots had to be counted in front of the Senate and the House of Representative in order for the vote to be official.

Martha was unhappy with her husband's new public role and would have rather stayed at Mount Vernon for the rest of her life. She decided that she would not travel to New York City with Washington but join him after he was settled into the presidential mansion.

Making matters worse, Washington discovered that he didn't have enough money to make the trip. He was rich in land, but poor in cash. He would have to borrow six hundred pounds from a friend to pay his travel expenses.

Finally, after more than a month of waiting and pacing and worrying, official word came on April 14, 1789, that he was elected president. On April 16th, he set out in his coach for New York City.

Cheering crowds welcomed Washington along the way to his inauguration.

Crowds cheered in every town and village that Washington passed through. Cannons roared in Baltimore and Wilmington. A congressional committee met him in Elizabethtown, New Jersey, for the final leg of his journey. Cannons fired a thirteen-gun salute when President Washington crossed New York Harbor in a barge manned by thirteen sailors—a symbol of the thirteen states. He landed at the foot of Wall Street and walked to his house on Cherry Street. Crowds shouted their approval. Tears of emotion streamed down Washington's cheeks.

On a sunny April 30, 1789, Washington stood on the balcony of Federal Hall and placed his trembling hand on a Bible. Congress, Vice President John Adams, and a huge crowd had come to hear him take the oath of office. "I do solemnly swear that I will faithfully execute the office of the president of the United States and will try, to the best of my ability, preserve, protect and defend the Constitution of the United States," Washington said. Although they were not part of the official oath, he added the words, "So help me God." Today, presidents still say those same words.

Robert R. Livingston, the chancellor of the state of New York turned to the crowd and said, "Long live George Washington, president of the United States." The people shouted back the words until it seemed as if the buildings were shaking from the sound. Cannons boomed in the harbor. Church bells rang. American liberty began its next journey.

"Mr. President"

Every detail of the new government had to be created. There was even a debate about what to call the president. Vice President John Adams suggested "His Elective Majesty" or "His Mightiness." A senator, when he finished laughing, said that Adams himself could be called "His Rotundity," as he was quite round. Eventually, the Senate decided that the president should simply be called "Mr. President." Washington certainly preferred "Mr. President" to "His Elective Majesty."

Washington wasn't happy living without Martha. He missed her and must have written to Mount Vernon to hurry her trip. His long-time secretary, Tobias Lear, also wrote to Martha. Washington's friends sent updates by mail and horsemen about her journey, so he could follow her progress.

Martha and her grandchildren, Nelly and Wash Custis, arrived in New York on

A statue on Wall Street in New York City marks the spot where George Washington was inaugurated as president.

Cornwallis, the Dog

When Washington traveled, he brought along his favorite greyhound dog, jokingly named Cornwallis after the English general. Cornwallis died on a southern trip and was buried on the banks of the Savannah River. Local residents kept up Cornwallis's marble tombstone for many years.

May 27. Three weeks later, Washington was stricken with a grave illness. A tumor on his left thigh had to be removed. It was common practice at the time for people to be kept awake during operations. There were no pain killers. For a few days, Washington's condition was critical. The street in front of the presidential mansion was roped off to prevent carriages from making noise. Straw was placed on the sidewalk to muffle the sound of footsteps. The president was not to be disturbed.

The surgery was a success, but forty days passed before Washington could return to his desk. When he did, one of his first tasks was to surround himself with the smartest and most experienced men in America. These men formed the first **cabinet**.

Two of the most important cabinet members were Alexander Hamilton, who was named **secretary of the treasury**, and Thomas Jefferson, who accepted the job of **secretary of state**. In choosing his most trusted advisers, Washington chose northerners and southerners, liberals and conservatives. He saw no reason why they couldn't pull together and work for the good of the country.

Congress's first order of business was a bill of rights. These ten amendments to the Constitution guaranteed basic rights like freedom of speech, of the press, and of religion.

Washington supported them.

As the first session of Congress drew to a close, Washington learned that his mother had died. Although the two didn't seem to get along, Washington was very sad to lose her.

Thomas Jefferson, Washington's secretary of state, would become the third President of the United States in 1801.

But there was no time to grieve. The president had promised to visit all the states of the union in his first term. In the fall of 1789, he made a month-long visit to New England. Two years later, in the spring of 1791, he toured the South. It's hard to believe today, but because the roads were bad and the mail moved slowly, Washington was completely out of touch with his government for two whole months. Luckily, Congress wasn't in session and nothing important happened while he was away.

Presidential Entertaining

Once Washington became president, he was too busy to have visitors come and go as they had at Mount Vernon. Soon he had an official schedule for entertaining. There were receptions for men every Tuesday from three to four, and official state dinners on Thursdays. Martha held tea parties on Friday evenings. Washington often dropped in to chat with the ladies.

Debates in Congress

Alexander Hamilton, Washington's secretary of the treasury, gained fame as a talented lawyer and eventually became leader of the Federal Party.

When Congress met for its second session in January 1790, Washington expected another busy and productive year. Two issues that they had to face were the question of where to place the permanent capital and how to repay Revolutionary War debts.

Alexander Hamilton tackled the second question. Hamilton had been Washington's aide-de-camp and personal secretary during the war. He was also a brilliant lawyer who understood finance and business. Hamilton had the knowledge to get the new country's finances in order. He worked on a plan to pay the country's debts and improve the economy. The plan called for the federal government to take over the war debts of individual states. States that had already paid their debts objected.

Virginia's James Madison led the arguments in Congress against Hamilton's plan. Thomas Jefferson, who had just joined the cabinet as secretary of state, presided over a deal: He supported Hamilton's financial plan. In exchange, Hamilton brought Jefferson the votes he needed to establish the nation's capital on a site along the Potomac River. Washington himself would choose the site and take over the planning of what was then called Federal City.

It was decided that Philadelphia would serve as the capital until the new city was ready.

The Washingtons arrived in Philadelphia on November 28, 1790. The presidential mansion was much bigger than the house in New York City, and Philadelphia was cleaner than New York. Perhaps that was because of the hogs that wandered the streets, acted as street cleaners! The Washingtons were frequent guests at Philadelphia's South Street Theater, where a stage box was reserved for the president.

The move to Philadelphia did nothing to change the mood in Congress. Thomas Jefferson and Alexander Hamilton continued to disagree about the direction that the country should take. This time, they didn't make a deal.

The move to Philadelphia did nothing to change the mood in Congress. Thomas Jefferson and Alexander Hamilton continued to disagree about the direction that the country should take.

The next step in Hamilton's financial plan called for a **national bank**. Jefferson opposed the bank, and his friend James Madison again led the arguments against it in Congress. Debates were long and fierce. Did Congress have the power to license a bank? Madison and Jefferson said no.

A split began to develop between those who believed that the government had only the powers that were spelled out exactly in the Constitution and those who believed that the Constitution suggested other powers.

Hamilton, who fought for a strong national government, was on one side. Jefferson, who thought the states should hold more power, was on the other. In this case, Hamilton's arguments were more persuasive. When Congress passed the bill authorizing the Bank of the United States, Washington signed it into law.

The conflict between Washington's trusted advisers got

There was no White House when George Washington was president. Instead, he and Martha lived in this house in Philadelphia, which was then the capital of the United States.

bigger. Their supporters split along geographic lines. Hamilton represented New York, a northern state, and believed government should be controlled by the merchant and banking class. Hamilton didn't trust popular rule. Jefferson, from the southern state of Virginia, wanted a democracy of farmers and workers. Jefferson put personal liberties above all. It was a division that would continue to grow. Jefferson came to believe that Hamilton was trying to restore a monarchy to the new nation. Eventually, Washington's support of Hamilton's financial plans would cause a break in the friendship between Jefferson and Washington. Newspapers on both sides attacked the other.

Only Washington was able to rise above the fighting. He listened to both sides. He tried to gather from each side the things that were most useful and important to the United States.

Washington feared for the unity of the new nation, but he still wanted to retire at the end of his first term. He explained that both his body and his mind were growing old. Washington believed that if he left office, Hamilton and Jefferson would try to work together for the good of the country. Washington didn't understand until that point just how violently the two men disagreed with each other.

Both Jefferson and Hamilton urged him to remain in office. "North and South will stay together," wrote Thomas Jefferson, only "if they have you to hang on." Washington saw that his nation still needed him, and he had no choice but to stay on.

Martha begged him to change his mind. George had long been promising her that he would retire at the end of his first term so they could return to Mount Vernon. She wished to be home surrounded by family and friends. But Washington again served his duty to his country. On February 13, 1793, the Electoral College unanimously elected him to a second term. This time, fifteen states took part in the voting—Vermont and Kentucky being the newest states to join the United States in 1791 and 1792 respectively.

Washington had no way of knowing that the biggest danger to his young country was taking shape across the ocean. A new revolution had begun, and it threatened to draw the United States into a world war.

Washington had no way of knowing that the biggest danger to his young country was taking shape across the ocean. A new revolution had begun, and it threatened to draw the United States into a world war.

CHAPTER 13

An Embattled Second Term

The unity of Government . . . is a main pillar in the edifice of your real independence.

On March 4, 1793, Washington was **inaugurated** for the second time. His second term was filled with one crisis after another. There were violent clashes between white settlers and Native Americans in the West, the French Revolution turned into the Reign of Terror, Pennsylvania farmers staged protests against a tax on whiskey, and Thomas Jefferson's battle with Alexander Hamilton ended only when Jefferson retired to Virginia at the end of 1793.

Hamilton and Jefferson both had followers who formed

The storming of the Bastille—a prison in Paris—marked the beginning of the French Revolution.

political societies. These societies became two separate political parties. The Hamiltonians evolved into the Federalist Party, who are today's Republicans; the Jeffersonians organized the Democratic-Republican Party, who are today's Democrats. The parties fought for their political beliefs in Congress and in the newspapers. The French Revolution caused one of their biggest disagreements.

Foreign Dilemma

In the first act of the French Revolution in 1789, Washington's good friend the Marquis de Lafayette joined in the storming of the Bastille—later sending one of the Bastille's famous keys to his former general as a tribute and a symbol of liberty. Washington hung it in the presidential mansion. Next to it, he added a portrait of King Louis XVI, the French king who had supported the American Revolution.

A key to the Bastille hangs in Mount Vernon today.

Just two weeks after his second inauguration, Washington took the picture down again when he learned that King Louis XVI had been beheaded. Now that they had toppled their own monarchy, the new leaders of France were determined to topple other European monarchies. France declared war on England, Spain, and Holland.

Most Americans, including Thomas Jefferson, believed that France's revolution was inspired by the American Revolution. Jefferson called on Washington to help the French rebels, but Washington vowed to do only what was best for the United States. He knew that a war with England would be disastrous for his new country and insisted that the United States remain neutral—"friendly and impartial."

Alexander Hamilton and the Federalists were horrified by the beheadings taking place in France. They believed that the United States needed to maintain trade with England. They accused Jefferson and the Republicans of trying to import the terrors of the French Revolution to the United States. The Republicans argued that the Federalists wanted to create a monarchy in America. Jefferson began to suspect that Washington himself might be a secret monarchist.

The United States would not have survived another war with Great Britain, and the revolution in France was out of control.

But history would prove Washington right. The United States would not have survived another war with Great Britain, and the revolution in France was out of control. At the time though, the American people sided with the French. Washington became a target of the Republican press. He was deeply hurt by the attacks, but he pretended to ignore them. Martha's own pain and anger on her husband's behalf were no secret.

Another crisis sprang up. In August 1793, Philadelphia was hit by the most deadly epidemic in American history. **Yellow fever** spread from ships to lodging houses and from neighborhood to neighborhood. No one understood that the disease was carried by mosquitoes. The number of dead just kept growing. Churches stopped ringing their bells for the dead in order to avoid panic.

John Jay came from a wealthy New York family.

Everyone who could—including most members of Congress—left Philadelphia for the countryside. Word came to Washington that his presence in the city was one of the few things that gave people hope, so he stayed. He tried to send Martha and his grandchildren to Mount Vernon, but Martha refused to leave without him. Eventually, the entire family left the city on September 10. Cold weather eventually put a stop to the epidemic.

Then trouble broke out with England. England tried to draw the United States into their war with France in the hopes of winning back some of their old empire. The British armed the Indian tribes in the West and ordered the British navy to seize American ships carrying French goods or headed for French ports. Captured American sailors were given two choices: join the British navy, or die on a prison ship.

The United States had to make peace with the British. Not only were they America's biggest trading partner, but British soldiers still manned forts in the western part of United States. Washington sent Supreme Court Justice John Jay to London to negotiate a treaty.

Jay sailed from New York on May 12, 1794. Washington could only wait and trust that Jay would act in the best interests of the nation. Washington did not know that Jay consulted secretly with Hamilton. Nor did he know that his ambassador to France, James Monroe, communicated secretly with Jefferson. By this time, Jefferson had resigned his cabinet post, and Hamilton would stay in government only for another year.

While Washington waited for word from England, he was faced with yet another crisis, this one in western Pennsylvania—strong opposition to a tax on whiskey. Resistance to the tax was so widespread that tax collectors were forced to run for their lives!

In August 1794, more than six thousand men gathered outside of Pittsburgh. They set up mock guillotines to show their support for the French Revolution, drank too much of their own whiskey, threatened to start their own nation, and dared the federal government to come after them.

Washington was outraged. Americans were free to protest, but in taking up arms, the protestors had gone too far. If citizens threatened to break away from the United States every time Congress passed a law they didn't like, the nation could not stand.

If citizens threatened to break away from the United States every time Congress passed a law they didn't like, the nation could not stand.

Washington took personal command of the thirteen thousand troops that were gathered to fight the protestors. They quickly backed down and the army was disbanded. The Whiskey Rebellion is the only time an American president led troops in battle while in office. The greatest crisis of Washington's presidency, though, was still to come.

The Jay Treaty

News traveled slowly in 1795. Washington was anxiously waiting for word from Jay in England. Unofficial rumors from ship captains and travelers indicated that a treaty with Britain had been negotiated. Washington knew that the Jeffersonians would hate the treaty the minute he received it, especially when he learned that Jay had said "to do more was not possible."

One positive thing was that the treaty called for British troops to leave the American frontier. But in every other way, the terms favored the British. The treaty gave America trade status with Great Britain but restricted American trade in the West Indies. Under the treaty, the British could still seize American ships headed for France, if they paid for the cargo. In Washington's view, the treaty accomplished his basic goal of avoiding a disastrous war with England, but others thought the trade restrictions were humiliating.

Washington called a special session of the Senate to ratify the

Treaties

In addition to the Jay Treaty, Washington signed two more important treaties before the end of his second term. The first was with Spain, which owned most of present-day Florida and Louisiana. The treaty gave United States citizens access to the Mississippi River and the Port of New Orleans. The Senate approved this treaty by a unanimous vote.

The second treaty was with the Shawnee, the Miami, and other Native Americans of the Northwest. The tribes gave up their claim to the Ohio River as their eastern boundary, and huge areas of Ohio and Indiana were opened to white settlers.

A mock representation of John Jay was hanged and burned by those angry about the Jay Treaty.

treaty. After sixteen days of fierce debate behind closed doors, the treaty was approved by a vote of twenty to ten. The Republican press, backed by Thomas Jefferson, bad-mouthed Washington and demanded that England be confronted—by declaring war, if necessary. The country was swept by violent protests against the treaty. Effigies, or insulting representations, of John Jay were created and burned all over the country.

When we look back today, we can see that the Jay Treaty improved trade and brought peace to North America. But at the time, it infuriated Washington's political enemies. Republicans thought that Washington had sold out to the British and turned his back on the French. Jefferson and his supporters turned their backs on Washington.

For eight years, Washington had led his country. He kept the new nation together, avoided a war that would have been disastrous, and opened up the gateways to the West. At the end of his second term, Washington was determined to step down. The nation would survive without him. He asked Alexander Hamilton to help him write his farewell to the American people.

Washington's farewell address was published in newspapers throughout the country in the fall of 1796. In it Washington declared that American independence, if it was to last, needed a strong unified government. It "is a main pillar in the edifice [structure] of your real independence," he wrote.

For eight years, Washington had led his country. He kept the new nation together, avoided a war that would have been disastrous, and opened up the gateways to the West.

Unlike in the first two presidential elections, in the third there was a contest between two political parties. As always, Washington stayed neutral, but he must have been relieved and happy when John Adams, a Federalist who believed in a strong government, was elected president. Thomas Jefferson, now Washington's enemy, received the second highest number of votes and was named vice president.

Martha and George couldn't wait to leave Philadelphia and public life forever. In March 1797, Washington turned the government over to Adams and Jefferson and went home to Mount Vernon. Finally, he would be able to live the life he longed for—that of a simple gentleman farmer.

Washington's Teeth

In Washington's time, people went to the dentist only to have their teeth pulled when they ached. Many people lost teeth, but Washington probably had a gum disease that made his tooth decay even worse. His teeth were black and rotted before he was in his early twenties. In the French and Indian War, the British made fun of his dental problems. He lost most of his teeth, and by the time he became president, he had only one tooth left. He had many sets of false teeth over the years, but none of them were wooden and none were made by Paul Revere.

Washington's first full set of false teeth was made of hippopotamus ivory and human teeth. Other sets included walrus and elephant ivory, and cow, elk, and human teeth. Most were held together with steel springs so powerful that Washington had to work hard to keep his mouth closed! They also made it hard to eat. Washington was often said to look unhappy at dinner parties.

Washington's clumsy dentures may have been the reason why he didn't make many public speeches.

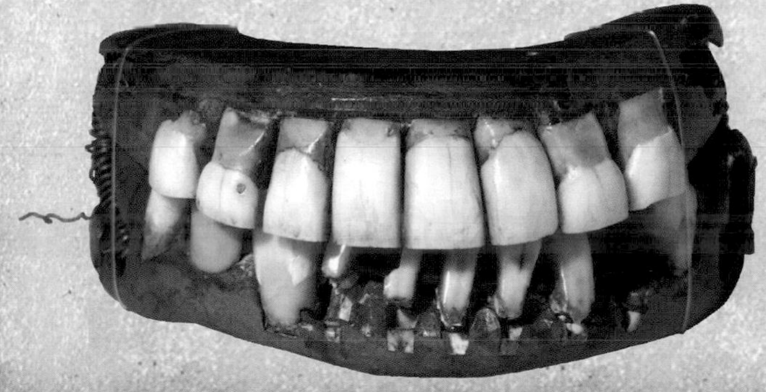

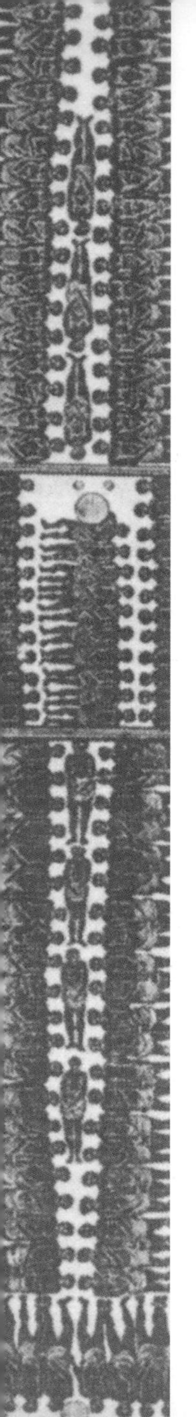

CHAPTER 14

Washington the Slave Owner

With this letter comes a Negro (Tom) which I beg the favour of you to sell, in any of the Islands you may go to, for whatever he will fetch . . .

George Washington's beliefs about slavery seem confusing and contradictory to us today. How could someone who led the fight for liberty also own slaves?

In Washington's time, slavery was a way of life in the South. He probably never questioned the fact that slaves cleaned his mother's house, worked his father's fields, and took care of him and his brothers and sisters.

When Washington's father died, eleven-year-old George inherited ten slaves along with Ferry Farm. After he married Martha and increased the size of Mount Vernon, Washington bought more slaves to work his new land. He was also responsible for the slaves on Martha's plantations.

At that stage in his life, there is no evidence that Washington had any second thoughts about owning other people. He talked about his slaves as if they were property. When they ran away, he posted notices and rewards so they would be captured and sent back.

Generally, slave quarters on plantations could be cold and uncomfortable. Families shared small log cabins. There was little furniture, a smoky fireplace, and a dirt floor. The workday was from sunup to sundown six days a week.

During the Revolution, Washington began to see black people in a new light. At first he was shocked to find African-Americans in the New England army. Washington told his officers to stop enlisting black soldiers. But Washington's army got smaller and smaller. He was desperate for new recruits and quietly changed his policy. Free black people were accepted into the fighting force. The Continental army was more **integrated** than any American army until the Vietnam War.

He was desperate for new recruits and quietly changed his policy. Free black people were accepted into the fighting force.

The British promised freedom to slaves who ran away to fight for the Redcoats. At the end of the war, Washington let Tories go free. But he insisted that those slaves who had run away to fight with the British be returned to their owners.

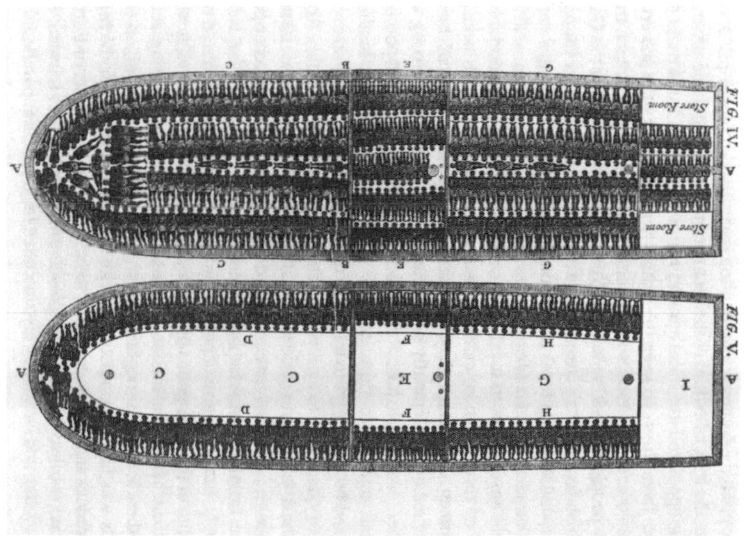

This cross-section shows the horrific and inhumane method of arranging human cargo on slave ships.

Rethinking Slavery

In the years at Mount Vernon between the war and the presidency, Washington began to question slavery. His slave population had grown to more than two hundred. There were more slaves than there was work to be done, and many of them were too old or too young to work.

Some of Washington's friends, including the Marquis de Lafayette, urged him to speak out against slavery. It was the next logical step in the American Revolution. Washington wasn't willing to take a public stand, but he wrote private letters to his friends saying that he wished slavery would be abolished—gradually.

When it came to his own slaves, though, Washington did not consider setting them free at this time. Washington owned only about one-third of his slaves. The rest belonged to Martha and

Billy Lee: George Washington's Valet

Washington's final instructions in his will concerned a slave named Billy Lee. Lee was George Washington's personal servant. He took care of his master's clothes and powdered and curled his hair. Lee was a strong horseman who joined Washington on foxhunts. During the American Revolution, Lee went to war with his master. He was in charge of Washington's most important papers and assumed unofficial command of the officers' servants. Washington freed Lee and granted him a pension of thirty dollars per year. Lee stayed at Mount Vernon for the rest of his life, entertaining visitors with stories about his adventures with General Washington.

Slave quarters at Mount Vernon

her heirs. Martha did not seem to share her husband's questioning attitude of slavery, and Washington was powerless to free her slaves.

He was also concerned about money. Because Washington had to support so many slaves, Mount Vernon could not make a profit. Almost all the crops grown on the farm were needed to feed the Washington family and the slaves. Washington came up with a plan not to free his slaves, but to sell them.

Did Washington believe that slavery was wrong? Or did he think that getting rid of slavery would have led to financial losses too great to bear? The answer isn't clear. He realized that selling his slaves would have destroyed their families, so he did not follow through on his plan.

At the Continental Congress, slavery caused the most bitter debate. The argument split the North and the South. Washington realized that the only way the country would come together was if slavery was left up to individual states. The Constitution of the United States failed to abolish slavery.

In 1790, two petitions before the House of Representatives argued for an end to slavery. Benjamin Franklin, the second-most admired man in America (President Washington was the first), supported the petitions. Debates in Congress were long and ugly. Again, the North and the South disagreed.

Did Washington share Benjamin Franklin's views? Washington did not speak out against slavery when he had the chance, maybe because his highest priority was to create a united

Benjamin Franklin opposed slavery.

Freedom and Liberty

Black soldiers adopted last names that declared why they were fighting. Many named themselves "Liberty" or "Freedom."

nation. He knew that slavery was the one issue that could destroy the new country. Washington was relieved when it was taken off the national agenda and made a state issue.

Eventually, Washington decided to free all his slaves. In July 1799, he locked himself in his study to write his will. To spare Martha, he wrote that his slaves should be freed only after her death. But she became convinced that some of the slaves wished her dead, so she freed her husband's 123 slaves on January 1, 1801.

Eventually, Washington decided to free all his slaves. In July 1799, he locked himself in his study to write his will. To spare Martha, he wrote that his slaves should be freed only after her death.

Some of the freed slaves stayed at Mount Vernon. Washington had ordered that the oldest slaves be clothed and fed as long as they lived. He also asked that the youngest slaves be supported until they were grown up. He wanted them to be taught how to read and instructed in a "useful occupation." Unfortunately, the state of Virginia passed laws against teaching black people to read and write, and that part of the will could not be carried out.

Washington was right about the states and slavery. It continued to be a wall between the North and the South. Eventually, it led to America's bloodiest war—the Civil War.

CHAPTER 15

First in the Hearts of His Countrymen

The remainder of my life, which in the course of nature cannot be long, will be occupied in rural amusements.

George and Martha's carriage drove up Mount Vernon's bell-shaped drive on March 15, 1797. Washington had written to his friend Henry Knox that he would spend the rest of his life "in rural amusements," but Mount Vernon had been neglected. There was much work to be done. Washington hired painters and carpenters to make repairs to the house. The farms and gardens were in need of attention, too. Washington complained about the mess, but Martha noted that he was clearly enjoying himself. She herself was thrilled to be home again. "We once more (and I am sure never to quit it again) got seated under our own roof," she wrote.

George Washington was pleased to resume life with Martha at Mount Vernon.

Amid the chaos of renovations, Washington's daily life was orderly. He got up at five o'clock every morning and read or wrote letters until his seven o'clock breakfast. Then he rode the rounds of his farms. He returned to the mansion for the midday meal, which sometimes lasted two hours.

The plantation house was busier than a hotel. Dignitaries and old friends visited. Everyone wanted to spend time with the most famous man in the country. Sometimes Washington didn't even know the names of all his guests.

Washington never did get the peace and quiet he said he longed for, but he was never happier than when he sat at his dining table surrounded by people. One day he realized that he and Martha had not sat down to dinner by themselves for more than twenty years! So many people arrived in his first year back home, that Washington asked his nephew, Lawrence Lewis, to come to Mount Vernon and act as host.

Two problems faced Washington in his retirement. The first was the question of what to do about his slaves. The second had to do with political news from Philadelphia.

Two problems faced Washington in his retirement. The first was the question of what to do about his slaves. The second had to do with political news from Philadelphia. The French were still at war with England. France disrupted American shipping in an attempt to force the United States into war. Washington feared that France and the Americans who supported the French cause would destroy the United States government still in its infancy.

Rumors spread that France was going to attack the United States. Congress raised an army and President John Adams appointed Washington commander in chief. Washington's acceptance reassured the nation, but he desperately hoped there would be no war. He left Mount Vernon for Philadelphia in November 1798 to organize a new army. Fortunately, the crisis was solved by diplomatic means. To Martha's relief, Washington returned to Mount Vernon after only six weeks.

"I am not afraid . . ."

On December 12, 1799, despite a storm that included snow, hail, and rain, Washington kept his regular routine. He rode his rounds for five hours, returning home wet and cold. Dinner was ready when he arrived. He didn't want to make his guests wait, so he did not change out of his wet clothes.

The next day, the weather was nasty again and Washington had a sore throat. He didn't make his daily rounds, but he walked the lawn and marked the trees he wanted cut down.

That night, Washington awoke Martha because he was having trouble breathing. Martha wanted to summon a

When he created this bust of George Washington, the artist Jean Antoine Hondon visited Mount Vernon and made a plaster cast of the former president's actual face.

Mount Rushmore, in South Dakota, pays tribute to presidents George Washington, Thomas Jefferson, Theodore Roosevelt, and Abraham Lincoln.

servant and a doctor, but Washington was afraid she would catch cold herself if she got out of bed. It wasn't until dawn, when a maid came to start the fire, that Washington sent for help. He was given a mixture of molasses, vinegar, and butter to soothe his throat, but he could not swallow a drop.

Medical treatments of the day included **bleeding and blistering**. Washington was bled more than four times. He got worse every time. Three doctors consulted at his bedside, but nothing they tried made it easier for Washington to breathe. He never complained or even talked about the pain he was in, but

George and Martha's Letters

After George's death, Martha burned their letters to each other. No one knows why. Perhaps they contained secrets. Or maybe Martha was tired of sharing her husband with the American people. Only three letters are known to have survived.

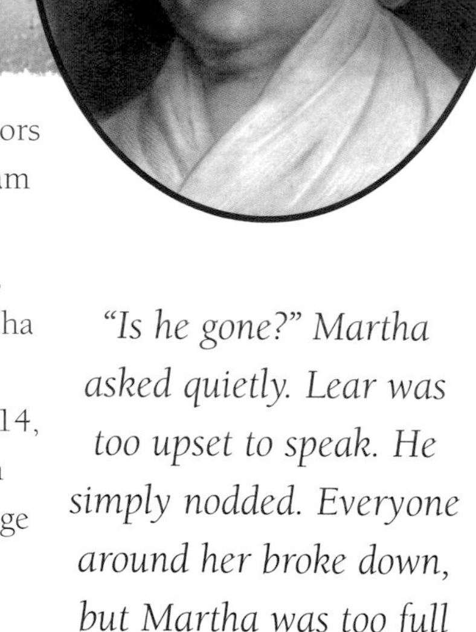

eventually Washington told the doctors to stop. "I die hard," he said, "but I am not afraid to go."

Washington's longtime secretary, Tobias Lear, was at his bedside. Martha never left his side. As the clock approached midnight on December 14, Washington withdrew his hand from Lear's and felt his own pulse. In charge until the very end, Washington took his last breath.

"Is he gone?" Martha asked quietly. Lear was too upset to speak. He simply nodded. Everyone around her broke down, but Martha was too full of grief to cry.

"Is he gone?" Martha asked quietly. Lear was too upset to speak. He simply nodded. Everyone around her broke down, but Martha was too full of grief to cry. She sent messages to the family and prepared for the funeral. After her husband died, Martha moved to a small third-floor bedroom. She closed for good Washington's study and the bedroom they had shared.

Family members gathered over the next three days. When the news of Washington's death reached Alexandria, Virginia, the

The Washington Monument was the world's tallest man-made structure when it was completed in 1884.

city's church bells started to toll and did not stop for four days. Two hundred soldiers wearing the uniform of the Virginia militia marched from Alexandria with a military band to take part in the funeral procession.

"Father, I Cannot Tell a Lie."

Shortly after George Washington's death, a parson named Mason Locke Weems published the first of his many biographies of the American hero. Not much was known about Washington's childhood, but that didn't worry Weems. He invented facts!

Weems made up a story about young George and a cherry tree. After George supposedly cut down the tree with his hatchet, he confessed the truth to his father with the words, "Father, I cannot tell a lie."

It became one of the most famous stories about young George Washington. More than two hundred years later, people still believe it.

A Nation Mourns

The cavalry led the procession, followed by soldiers with their weapons reversed. The band beat muffled drums. Washington's riderless horse was led by black-clad servants. Martha was too upset to take part in the procession, to talk, or to cry. She sat alone in her bedroom. She must have heard the shots from the soldiers' muskets after the door of Washington's tomb was sealed.

The nation mourned, too. Congress did not learn of Washington's death until December 18—four days later. Members of the Senate sent a note to President John Adams that read, "Our country mourns her father." Four thousand people attended the memorial service in Philadelphia. Henry "Light-Horse Harry" Lee delivered one of two eulogies. His description of Washington is still true today: "First in war, first in peace, and first in the hearts of his countrymen."

Processions, ceremonies, and speeches continued throughout the nation for more than two months after Washington's death.

Processions, ceremonies, and speeches continued throughout the nation for more than two months after Washington's death. Cities, states, and monuments were named in honor of him. Many great speakers praised the president, but nothing would have made him happier than these simple words: George Washington, American.

Glossary

allegiance—loyalty that a person feels to his or her country.

bleeding and blistering—pre-scientific "cures" that required deliberate bleeding or blistering to the body so certain illnesses could "escape."

boycotts—deliberate acts to avoid communicating with or purchasing from a group in order to express disapproval.

cabinet—a group of advisers appointed by the head of state to run the executive departments of the government.

Continental army—military force—made up of men from the thirteen colonies—that fought against the British in the American Revolution.

Continental Congress—meetings of colonial representatives in 1774, 1775, and 1776 to establish laws that formed the United States of America.

delegates—representatives authorized to attend a conference or convention.

Electoral College—delegates from each state (called electors) who formally vote to elect the president and vice president of the United States.

inaugurated—assumed office by taking a solemn oath.

integrated—opened to all racial groups for full participation.

militia—an army made up of citizen volunteers.

national bank—a bank under the supervision of the federal government.

propaganda—information given out to deliberately further one's own cause or damage the opposition's cause.

ratify—formally approve or make valid.

repeal—to revoke or take back an act or law.

secretary of state—a cabinet head that is responsible for conducting foreign policy.

secretary of the treasury—a cabinet head that is responsible for all finance and monetary matters.

surveyor—a person who uses special measuring tools to determine the boundaries of specific land areas.

Tories—a resident of the thirteen colonies who favored maintaining the autority of the British monarchy during the American Revolution. Also called Royalists.

treaty—a written agreement between two or more groups or countries.

yellow fever—a deadly disease usually occurring in hot tropical climates and caused by a virus transmitted by a mosquito bite.

Bibliography

Books

Bober, Natalie S. *Countdown to Independence*. New York: Atheneum Books for Young Readers, 2001.

Brady, Patricia. *Martha Washington: An American Life*. New York: Viking, 2005.

Davis, Kenneth C. *Don't Know Much About History*. New York: HarperCollins, 2003.

Ellis, Joseph J. *His Excellency: George Washington*. New York: Alfred A. Knopf, 2004.

Fleming, Thomas. *Liberty! The American Revolution*. New York: Viking, 1997.

Flexner, James Thomas. Washington: *The Indispensable Man*. New York: Little, Brown and Company, 1974.

McCullough, David. *1776*. New York: Simon & Schuster, 2005.

Articles

Ellis, Joseph J. "Washington Takes Charge." *Smithsonian* (January 2005): [p 92].

Ewers, Justin. "Washington's Proving Ground." *U.S. News and World Report* (April 2004) : [p 68].

Ferling, John. "The Final Days." *American History*(December 1999) : [p 42].

Fleming, Thomas. "George Washington, Spymaster." *American Heritage* (February 2000) : [p 45].

Gelb, Norman. "Winter of Discontent." *Smithsonian* (May 2003) : [p 64].

"Honoring Courage." *Smithsonian* (November 2004) : [p 40].

Meacham, Jon. "History: Rethinking Washington." *Newsweek* (May 23, 2005) : [p 38-45].

Shore, Diane ZuHone. "Presidential Dentures." *Highlights for Children* (February 2002) : [p 16].

Smith, Richard North. "The Surprising George Washington." *The U.S. National Archives & Records Administration* (Spring 1994).

Triber, Jane. "George Washington." *American Eras*, (Gale Research, 1997–1998).

About the Author

Laurie Calkhoven is a children's writer and editor living in New York City. In addition to Mount Vernon and Washington's headquarters in Morristown, she visited some famous New York City sites while researching George Washington's life, including Fraunces Tavern and Federal Hall, where Washington was inaugurated.

Image Credits

Photo by Szpak Astoria: 84 (left)

Photo by Maehl Billings: 84 (right)

The Colonial Williamsburg Foundation: 18

© CORBIS: 46

© Bettmann/CORBIS: 55

© Gianni Dagli Orti/CORBIS: 97

Painting by Don Troiani, www.historicalartprints.com: 54

Florida Center for Instructional Technology: 39

The Granger Collection, New York: 6, 10, 12, 14, 17, 21, 22, 24 (bottom), 26, 29, 31 (top and bottom), 33, 44, 45, 53, 56, 57, 59, 61, 62, 63, 75, 80, 82, 89, 95, 100, 103, 112

Courtesy of Hunt Institute for Botanical Documentation, Carnegie Mellon University, Pittsburgh, PA: 3

Independence National Historical Park: 83,

Library of Congress: 7, 9, 24 (top), 37, 41, 42, 49, 72, 73, 78, 110, 116, 118

Photo by Chris McKenna: 90

Photo courtesy of the Military & Historical Image Bank: 51

Courtesy of Mount Vernon Ladies' Association: 2, 8, 11, 28, 77, 79, 98, 105, 109, 114

National Archives and Records Administration: 70, 85

Photo by Walton Portsmouth: 84 (middle)

Photo by Nicolas Raymond: 117

South Dakota Tourism: 115

Virginia Department of Historic Resources: 4-5

Wikipedia, The Free Encyclopedia: 30, 35, 40, 48, 64, 68, 76, 86, 92, 93, 107,

The Winterthur Museum, Garden and Library: 74

Cover art: Brooklyn Museum/ Corbis

Index